THE
WEEKEND
DECORATOR

THE
WEEKEND
DECORATOR

GINA MOORE
AMY DAWSON

A Dorling Kindersley Book

Dorling Kindersley

LONDON, NEW YORK, SYDNEY, DELHI,
PARIS, MUNICH, and JOHANNESBURG

Created and produced by
C&B Packaging Limited

Managing Editor Kate Yeates
Project Editor Jinny Johnson
Art Director Roger Bristow
Art Editor Helen Collins
Designer Anne Fisher
Styled Photography Lucinda Symons
Step Photography Brian Hatton, Sampson Lloyd
Stylist Ali Edney
Set Builder Stephen Gott
Illustrator David Ashby

Published in the United States by
Dorling Kindersley Publishing, Inc.
95 Madison Avenue,
New York, New York 10016

First American Edition, 2000
2 4 6 8 10 9 7 5 3 1

ISBN 0-7894-6129-3

Printed and bound in China
by L Rex Printing Co. Ltd

see our complete
catalogue at
www.dk.com

CONTENTS

INTRODUCTION

With the fast pace of life today there never seems to be the time to make those home improvements which feel so necessary. Yet as *The Weekend Decorator* shows, furniture, windows, even a whole room can be transformed in just a weekend, if not a few hours.

The time-conscious projects are also stylish and require no special skills. The step-by-step instructions will guide you through the projects, and any further information you will need is explained and illustrated in the chapters on basic techniques.

Each project has a guide to the time it will take at the top of the page, so that you will know at a glance how many hours to set aside for it. The time given is the actual time needed for working on the project. It assumes you have done any necessary preparation such as taking measurements for calculating curtain fabric or preparing a wall for painting, and organized all your materials and bought the fabric, paint, or other items needed. Each project starts with an itemized list of tools and materials. Make sure you have all at hand before you start – otherwise you may find yourself stuck half way through a project with a vital piece of material missing.

Paint projects

One of the easiest ways to transform a room is to give it a coat of paint. Paint is cheap, easy to obtain, and straighforward to apply. A simple colorwash can give a room a whole new personality. With a little more effort you can achieve exciting effects, such as stenciling, stamping, or trompe l'oeil panels. Alternatively, try some of the furnishing projects. Transform your kitchen cabinet doors with a Shaker-look dragged effect, or paint some old frames with crackle glaze. A thrift-shop find can become a gleaming lacquered cabinet or an old lawn chair be given a new lease of life with a verdigris effect.

Thorough preparation

For the best results, always prepare thoroughly before starting a project. When you are short of time it may be tempting to cut corners, but you will always regret it and rushing may cost time in the end. Make sure walls are clean and free of grease and dust before you start. Fill any cracks and sandpaper over any rough patches. Clear the room of as much furniture as possible and cover any items that cannot be moved. If you are doing a project with a design such as stripes or checks, measure the area carefully first to check how well the design fits your wall and adapt if necessary. Furniture, whether new or old, should be stripped of paint if necessary and always sanded and wiped clean to provide a good, even surface for the paint to adhere to.

If you are trying a special paint effect such as stippling or stenciling for the first time, experiment first on some lining paper and practise the technique until you feel confident. Choose paint colors carefully. Many manufacturers now supply sample pots you can take home and try out before making up your mind. Be sure to buy enough paint for the job as different batches won't always match. Most

manufacturers provide guidelines on the tin. If you mix glazes yourself, keep note of the different colors and quantities you use in case more has to be mixed.

Fabric projects

If you feel like working with fabric rather than paint, the soft furnishing projects in this book can be used to add color, comfort, and a dash of style to every room in your home. You may choose to frame your windows with elegant curtains, or more simply with a classic shade. You may be inspired to transform your bedroom with a dramatic canopy, or revamp a headboard with a padded cover. There are quilts, cushions, and storage solutions from which to draw inspiration and, with a little thought, all of them can be adapted to suit your own particular needs.

First, choose your fabric.

You will find that there is a vast array available and it is important to take time when making your selection to make sure the fabric is right for the room and the project. Ask for sample swatches of the fabrics that catch your eye. Take them home and look at them in situ, both in daylight and artificial light. Look at the color and pattern, and try to imagine the impact, either subtle or daring, the fabrics would have on your room. Consider their weight, texture, and the way they behave – do they drape beautifully for a curtain or throw? Does the feel of the fabric lend itself to a cushion or quilt? Will it be strong enough for a loose cover? Finally you should think about aftercare: will the fabric shrink when washed, or will the colors fade?

Take care to measure and estimate properly. Study the instructions in the techniques section on measuring and estimating fabric. Read the guidelines for the particular project you are going to do thoroughly before you start. There is nothing worse than clearing the decks for a weekend of creative endeavor, only to find out that you have underestimated the amount of fabric you need. When in doubt, buy more than you think you need – any leftover fabric can be used to trim another project!

Be inspired

Remember that all the projects in this book are essentially quick and simple and well within your capabilities, however much you doubt them. You don't need any special skills so don't let yourself be put off. Clear a space to work and begin. You will be amazed at how enjoyably your weekend will pass. At the end, you will look on your handiwork with pride – and start to plan your next weekend project!

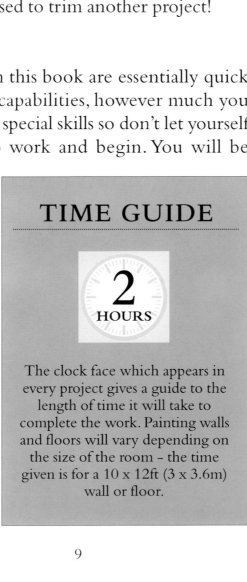

TIME GUIDE

2 HOURS

The clock face which appears in every project gives a guide to the length of time it will take to complete the work. Painting walls and floors will vary depending on the size of the room – the time given is for a 10 x 12ft (3 x 3.6m) wall or floor.

9

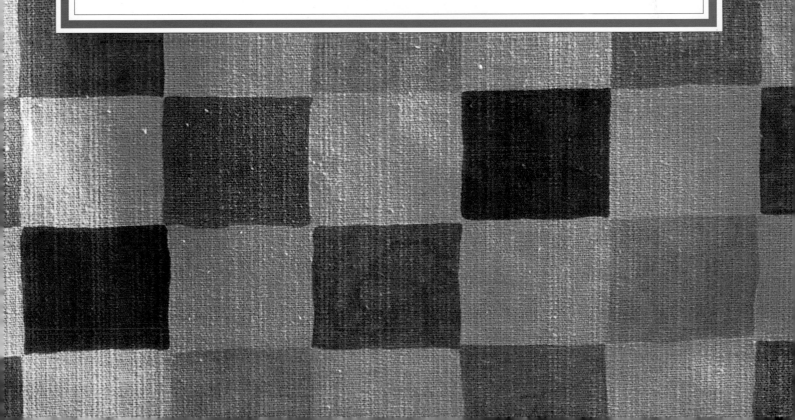

HALLS

STONE BLOCKS

Dramatic effect • Adds texture • Creates grandeur

PAINTED STONE blocks give a cool airy feeling and help create an illusion of space in a room. They look best in an area such as a hall, where there is usually a minimum of furniture and clutter to conflict with their clean lines. The wall is first colorwashed in a creamy yellow shade and the brush marks softened with a dry brush. Once you have figured out the size of the blocks you want, they are marked on the wall lightly in pencil. Finally, the pencil lines are carefully painted over with brown acrylic paint and highlighted in white.

Cool sophistication *A look of cool sophistication is brought to this hall by the use of painted stone blocks. The colorwash ground gives an impression of texture, while the lines break up a long wall.*

PROJECT PLANNER

Tools and Materials

Cream or pale yellow vinyl flat latex • Ready-mixed buff or creamy-yellow colorwash, or mix your own with raw umber artist's acrylic and scumble glaze (see p.165) • Raw umber artist's acrylic • White artist's acrylic • Roller and tray • Paintbrush • Small artist's brush • Softening brush • Cheese cloth • Ruler • Pencil • Carpenter's level

3½ HOURS

1 *Prepare the wall (see p.169). Using a roller, apply a coat of cream or pale yellow vinyl flat emulsion. The yellower the color of this base, the warmer the stone effect will look. Let it dry for 30 minutes.*

2 *Take the ready-mixed colorwash or mix your own (see p.165). Working in sections (see p.170), start to apply the colorwash with the paintbrush. Use rough crisscrossing strokes and let the coverage be lighter in some places, giving an uneven cover.*

3 *While the paint on the first section of wall is still wet, take a piece of mutton cloth, bunch it up in your hand, and lightly dab over the wall, softening and lifting the paint. This removes some of the bigger brush strokes.*

4 *Then take a dry softening brush and brush over the area to soften the brush marks further. Repeat Steps 2 to 4 until the wall is complete.*

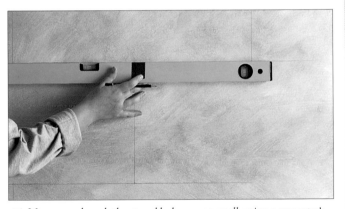

5 *Measure and mark the stone blocks on your wall, using a carpenter's level to check that lines are straight. The rows should be staggered as in a real stone wall. (See p.176 for more information on measuring and marking stone blocks.) The blocks here are 12 x 24in (30 x 60cm).*

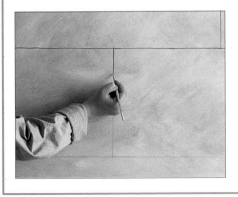

6 *Mix some raw umber acrylic paint with a small amount of white acrylic to soften it slightly. Using a small artist's brush, carefully hand paint over the pencil lines marking the blocks. Start at the top and work down.*

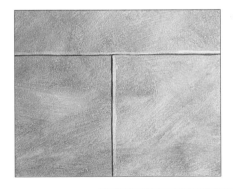

7 *Using white acrylic, highlight the brown lines. Work to the right of vertical lines and above horizontal lines. The white lines do not have to go right along each line – they look best if they are slightly broken and uneven.*

SHADE WITH TIES

Sculptural simplicity • Makes a decorative screen • No complicated cord system

DECORATIVE RATHER than functional, this shade is most suitable for a hall or stairway window, where there is no need for it to be raised too often. It looks best at least half lowered and makes a useful screen for an unappealing view, such as a busy street or a plain brick wall. The fabric is unlined to let maximum light through when it is lowered.

The shade is simply slotted onto a pole. This should extend at least 6in (15cm) on each side of the window frame, since the ties will pull the fabric slightly inward.

Allow at least 8in (20cm) extra in the length of the shade to give the pleats fullness even when the shade is lowered.

Choose a fabric that is light but has enough body to hold the shape of the shade. The example here is made from closely woven mercerized cotton, with a slightly stiff texture. Silk taffeta or shantung would also be a good choice, although silk should always be lined. Consider using a bold pattern – since so much flat fabric is on display, any design is shown off to full advantage. The ties here have been cut across the width of the fabric for contrast.

Graceful pleats

This shade's sculptural beauty lies in its simplicity. There is no complicated cord system, and the fabric is simply pleated up by hand and held in place with loosely knotted ties. The fabric then falls gracefully at each side. To lower the shade completely, simply undo the ties and let it fall to its full length. Here the ties have been made from the same fabric as the shade, but a plain or contrasting fabric could also be used.

PROJECT PLANNER

2 HOURS

Tools and Materials

Main fabric: length of window plus 4in (10cm) for slot at top plus ¾in (2cm) for base hem and 8in (20cm) for fullness x width of window plus 6in (15cm) on each side and 1½in (4cm) for side hems (see p.129 for information on measuring windows) • Two straight ties (see p.146), each with a finished width of 2in (5cm) x twice the length of shade • Curtain pole • Sewing machine and thread to match fabric

1 *Press and pin ⅜in (1cm) double hems on both sides and the base of the shade. Machine-stitch hems in place.*

2 *At the top of the shade, press over ⅜in (1cm) then 3½in (9cm) and pin in place. This forms a casing for the pole.*

4 *Machine stitch the ties in place on the fold line, backstitching at the start and finish to secure.*

3 *Make ties (see p.146). Place fabric right side up on the table, opening out the 3½in (9cm) fold at the top. Take one tie and mark the center point of its length. Place the tie about 12in (30cm) from the side edge of the shade with the center point on the pressed fold line and pin. Position the second tie 12in (30cm) from other side of the shade the same way.*

5 *Place the shade wrong side up and refold the top to form a casing for the pole. Pin and machine-stitch close to the folded edge, making sure the ties are well out of the way and do not get caught in the stitching. Once the shade has been put up, check the length of the ties, trim if necessary, and finish the ends by hand.*

WOODGRAINED DOOR

Transforms a door • Creates character • Adds a feature

THIS SIMPLIFIED version of woodgraining transforms an ordinary flat door into a thing of beauty and adds character to your hall or foyer. Before you start, study the look of real wood to give you an idea of the form of grain and knot marks.

The door is painted pale yellow and then given a coat of umber glaze. The glaze is dragged and softened, and knot and grain marks are added with a sharpened cork. These marks are also softened, and the door is finished with a coat of varnish for protection. Base boards and items of furniture can also be given this treatment.

Vary the color of the glaze according to the wood you wish to imitate – a rich deep shade for mahogany, for example, or a lighter one for pine.

Perfect painting
Sharpen your woodgraining skills before you start painting the door by practicing on a spare piece of wood.

PROJECT PLANNER

2¾ HOURS

Tools and Materials

Pale yellow vinyl flat latex • Raw umber artist's acrylic • Scumble glaze • Satin or gloss polyurethane varnish • Roller and paint tray • Paintbrushes • Sandpaper • Cork • Knife • Dragging brush • Softening brush • Brush for varnish

1 Sand the door. Using a roller, apply a coat of pale yellow vinyl flat latex all over the surface of the door. Use a brush to finish the inside edges of panels. Let it dry for 30 minutes.

2 Mix a glaze with raw umber artist's acrylic and scumble glaze (see p. 165). Apply the glaze to the center panel of the door. Drag the paint down the door with smooth, even brush movements.

3 With a dry dragging brush, drag over the glaze. Gently twitch your arm occasionally to break the lines slightly. With a softening brush, gently brush over the glaze to further soften the dragging lines (see inset).

4 Sharpen one end of the cork. Use it to make knot and grain marks to imitate the look of the real wood. Work down the door while it is wet, repeating patterns.

5 Using a softening brush and extremely light vertical strokes, gently brush out the marks to make the lines more subtle. Repeat Steps 2 to 5 on the lower panel of the door.

6 Repeat Steps 2 to 5 on the stiles. Work down vertical stiles and across horizontal stiles. Follow the order for painting a door given on p. 171.

7 When the glaze is dry, finish the door with a coat of satin polyurethane varnish. If you want a high shine, use gloss varnish instead.

CONTRAST-LINED DOOR CURTAIN

Keeps out drafts • Looks warm and welcoming • Brightens two rooms

A DOOR CURTAIN can serve as a draft stopper and helps give a welcoming look to a hallway. Here an embroidered natural linen fabric makes an elegantly muted statement while the flamboyant red check on the reverse presents an entirely different face to the adjoining room. The heading is unstiffened in keeping with the relaxed nature of the curtain. A fabric tieback, attached to a hook by the doorway, holds the curtain back for access. If there is room at the side of the door, use a wider pole so the curtain can be pulled right out of the way if necessary.

Elegant door curtain *Look for fabrics that work well together, not only in pattern and color, but also in weight. A flimsy fabric would sag and pull if teamed with a much heavier material.*

PROJECT PLANNER

3 HOURS

Tools and Materials

Main fabric: length of door plus 1½in (4cm) for base hem and 4in (10cm) for top hem x twice the width of pole, plus 1½in (4cm) for side seam allowances, joining widths if necessary (see p.129) • Contrast fabric: as main fabric • Tieback (see p.149): cut one 8 x 31½in (20 x 80cm) in either fabric • Curtain hooks, one for every 4in (10cm) of fabric and one for each end • Curtain pole and rings (same number as hooks) • Sewing machine and thread to match fabric

1 *Place main fabric and contrast fabric right sides together and pin at the sides, leaving a ¾in (2cm) seam allowance. Machine-stitch side seams, leaving the bottom 3in (7.5cm) of the fabric open.*

2 *Turn the curtain right side out. At the bottom, turn 1½in (4cm) hems on both lengths of fabric to the inside of the curtain. Press and pin in place.*

3 *Using even slipstitch (see p.138), sew the folded edges at the base of the curtain together, making sure you finish the open edges above the corners on each side.*

4 **Turn over a double 2in** *(5cm) hem at the top of the curtain, folding the main fabric over the contrast fabric. Press*

5 *Work out how many curtain hooks you need. Allow one for each end and arrange the rest at even intervals roughly 4in (10cm) apart across the curtain top. Using couching stitch (see p.139), attach each hook ½ in (12mm) below the curtain top. Attach each hook firmly, adding a few stitches at the top to keep it from flopping forward (see p.139).*

6 *Make a stiffened tieback (see p.149), with a finished width of 3½in (9cm). Stitch a ring to each end on the wrong side to attach the tie to a hook on the wall to hold the curtain back.*

GILDED UMBRELLA STAND

Instant glamour • Easy embellishment • Adds discreet note of sophistication

GILDING IS A relatively simple way of adding a touch of luxury to a simple item of furniture. Here we have gilded a plain wooden umbrella stand, but the technique could be used on a wooden chest, a small table, or a lamp base. The design is traced onto the item, and gold size is applied to the inside of the shape. The edges of the sized area must be as straight as possible since they will determine the shape of the gold leaf, which is laid over the size. The excess gold is very carefully brushed away, leaving the gleaming gilded shape.

Glamorous gilding *Simple shapes give the most successful results for gilding. Look for details, such as the top edge of this umbrella stand, that can also be gilded for extra effect.*

PROJECT PLANNER

5½ HOURS

Tools and Materials
Vinyl flat latex • Gold leaf • Gold size • Varnish
• Tracing paper • Pencil • Small square-ended
paintbrush • Small paintbrush • Brush for varnish
• Facial tissue

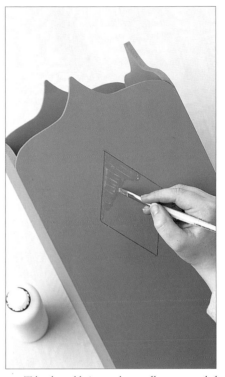

1 *Sand the item and prepare the surface if necessary (see p. 168). Apply two coats of vinyl latex in your chosen color, leaving each to dry for 30 minutes.*

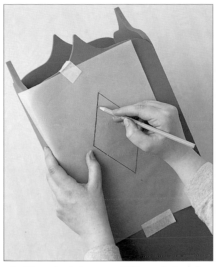

2 *Copy the design on p. 178 or a design of your choice onto tracing paper. Center the design on the item and secure it with masking tape. Go over the line in pencil to transfer it to the wood.*

3 *Take the gold size and a small square-ended paintbrush. Apply size to the inside of the traced shape, making sure the edges are as straight as possible.*

4 *Gold leaf must be handled very gently. Take a piece that will more than cover your shape. Lay the gold leaf onto the shape and gently smooth it down with a small piece of tissue and your finger so it sticks to the sized area.*

5 *Using a clean brush, with the greatest care, brush away the excess gold to leave the gilded shape. Repeat Steps 2 to 5 to make as many gilded shapes as you need. Here the top edge of the stand is also gilded with little scraps of gold leaf. Leave to dry thoroughly.*

6 *Apply a coat of flat or gloss varnish, depending on the finish you want. Varnish the painted and gilded areas.*

CONSOLE TABLE COVER

Conceals an old table • Elegant and practical • Provides hidden storage area

WITH A STYLISH full-length fabric cover, a basic table or shelf system in the hall becomes not only a useful surface, but also provides a concealed storage area underneath. If you do not have a table of a suitable size for your hall, a simple structure can be made from blockboard. It is important to take measurements very carefully and to allow ¼in to ⅜ (5mm to 1cm) of ease to every dimension when you cut out the fabric panels. If the cover fits the table too tightly, it will not hang well at the corners.

A simple shape *The skirts of the cover are split at the front corners and are held in place with fabric ties. Use upholstery-weight fabrics with enough body to hang well over such a simple shape.*

PROJECT PLANNER

2½ HOURS

Tools and Materials

Main fabric: measure the table. Cut two panels the width and height of the table, plus ⅜in (4cm) seam allowance all around; cut two side panels the depth and height of the table, plus ⅜in (4cm) seam allowance all around; cut one top panel to fit the top, plus 1½in (4cm) seam allowance
• Ties: cut 8 bias strips to make ties with a finished width of ¾ x 10in (2 x 25cm) (see p.148)
• Sewing machine and thread to match or contrast with fabric

1 *Place a side panel and front panel right sides together, aligning them at the top edges, and pin. Making a ¾in (2cm) seam allowance, machine stitch down to 5in (12.5cm) from the top. Backstitch to secure stitching firmly. Repeat to attach the remaining side panel to the other edge of the front panel. Attach the back panel to the free edges of the side panels, stitching all the way down to the base hem.*

2 *Press the seams open. Press under double ⅜in (1cm) hems along the raw edges at the front and around the bottom hem.*

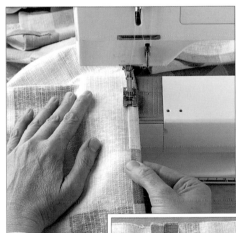

4 *Pin the top panel to the skirt, leaving a ¾in (2cm) seam allowance. When you get to a corner, clip the seam allowance so you can separate the edges to make a right angle (see p.136). Leaving the needle in the work, lift the foot and pivot the work. Lower the foot again and continue stitching down next side.*

3 *Machine-stitch all around double side hems and the base hem. When you reach the seam, lift the foot, turn the work, lower the foot, and stitch across the seam. Repeat to turn the work again and continue stitching down the other side. Clip the seam allowance just above the stitching so the seam lies flat (see inset).*

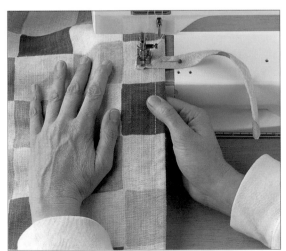

5 *Make 8 bias ties (see p.148). Finish one end of each tie. Tucking the unfinished end under, pin a tie to the right side of the front panel about one third of the way down from the top and 1in (2.5cm) in from the line of machine stitching. Machine stitch in place (see p.146). Stitch a second tie two-thirds of the way down from the top. Stitch matching ties to the adjoining panel. Repeat to stitch ties at the other side of the front panel.*

STAINED FLOORBOARDS

Disguises shabby floorboards • Practical • An inexpensive contemporary look

A QUICK AND EASY way of creating interesting flooring, staining can look spectacular and help to cover inexpensive or imperfect floorboards. Any shade of stain can be used to coordinate with the color scheme of your room.

The finished look of light, medium, and dark boards is achieved by using one, two, or three coats of stain on the appropriate boards. Mark each board clearly before you start so that you do not get confused once you begin the masking and staining process.

A different look *A rich blue stain makes a refreshing change from the usual wood-look shades used on floors and gives this hall a dynamically different look.*

PROJECT PLANNER

5 HOURS

Tools and Materials
Woodstain • Polyurethane varnish • Low-tack masking tape • Sandpaper • Paintbrushes

1 *If the floorboards are painted or treated in any way, strip and sand them before staining. If they are untreated, simply sand them to remove any roughness and make sure they are free of wax and grease.*

2 *Using a brush, apply one coat of stain over all the floorboards. Leave for 30 minutes or until touch dry.*

3 *The aim is to make alternating dark, medium, and light boards by applying one, two, or three coats of stain. Using low-tack masking tape, mask the inside edges of all boards that are to have the lightest finish.*

4 *Apply a second coat of stain to the boards that are to be medium and dark. Leave until touch dry as before.*

5 *Apply low-tack masking tape to the inside edges of medium boards. (You don't need to mask edges next to light boards.) Apply a third coat of stain to the boards that are to be the darkest. Leave to dry.*

6 *Gently remove the masking tape, taking care not to remove any stain. Apply a coat of polyurethane varnish to all the boards.*

LIVING ROOMS

PEARLY STRIPES

Cool contemporary style • Easily achieved elegance • Adds a glamorous touch

PEARLY PAINT lends an instant touch of glamour and style to any room. Try painting a room in these stripes or decorate just one wall for a more subtle look. The wall is painted in the base color first, and the stripes are then measured and marked. Every other stripe is masked off and painted in the pearly finish, leaving the stripes in between the base color.

Always use low-tack masking tape for masking stripes like these, or you are in danger of pulling off paint when you remove the tape.

An elegant sheen *The lustrous sheen of these pearly stripes makes a perfect backdrop to modern furnishings and brings light and vivacity to your living room.*

PROJECT PLANNER

4 ¼ HOURS

Tools and Materials
Vinyl flat latex in base color • Pearly metallic paint in stripe color • Paintbrush • Mini-roller • Low-tack masking tape • Pencil • Ruler • Carpenter's level

1 *Prepare the wall (see p. 169) and apply vinyl flat latex in the base color all over the area (see p. 166). Leave it to dry for about 30 minutes.*

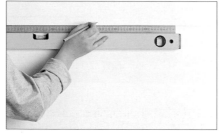

2 *Measure the wall and divide into horizontal stripes (see p. 175). The stripes here are 8in (20cm) wide. Mark the stripes lightly in pencil, using a level to make sure they are straight.*

3 *Using low-tack masking tape, mask alternate stripes to be painted in the metallic color. Place the tape very carefully along the outside edges of the stripes to be painted with metallic paint. (The stripes between remain in the base color.)*

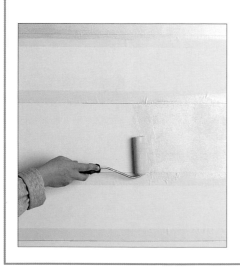

4 *Using a mini-roller, apply a coat of metallic paint to the masked stripes. Make sure you work right up to the masking tape and get paint to go over the tape. Leave this first coat to dry thoroughly for 30 minutes and apply a second coat.*

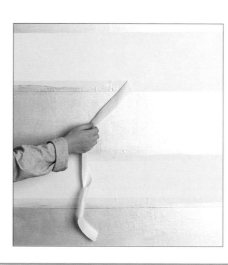

5 *When the stripes are complete, gently peel off the masking tape.*

ENVELOPE PILLOWS

Add comfort and color • Quick and simple to make • Range of finishes

PILLOWS GIVE an instant dash of personality to a room, adding color, texture, and a welcoming touch. The simple envelope cover is like a European-style pillowcase and is made from one length of fabric folded to form a pocket, with an inside flap that holds the pillow form in place. Once you have mastered this simple construction, vary the covers by making the length of fabric out of separate pieces, so the main cover and flap are different colors, and by adding finishing touches such as buttons and ties to hold the cover closed.

Coordinating pillows *Pick fabrics that reflect the simple nature of the covers, such as plain linens and silk or checked or striped cotton. Choose a range of two or three colors that work well together.*

PROJECT PLANNER

3 HOURS

Tools and Materials

Three pillow forms 18 x 18in (45 x 45cm) • Fabric for one of each pillow (covers should fit snugly so do not add seam allowances): three main panels 18 x 36in (45 x 90cm); three contrast flaps 8 x 18in (20 x 45cm); one contrast strip 3½ x 18in (9 x 45cm) • Fabric for two straight ties (see p.146) with a finished size of 1½ x 4in (4 x 25cm) • Three buttons • Length of iron-on interfacing 2¾ x 18in (7 x 45cm) • Sewing machine and thread to match fabric

Envelope pillow

1 *Place the contrast flap along the top edge of the main panel, right sides together, and pin. Machine stitch ⅝in (1.5cm) from the raw edges. Press. Press over a ⅜in (1cm) double hem at each end of the cover and pin. Machine stitch in place (see inset).*

2 *Fold the main panel in half and fold the contrast flap down over the main panel. Pin the side seams together. Machine stitch 1.5in (⅝cm) from the raw edges, starting at the top of the contrast panel. Turn the cover right side out.*

Envelope pillow with ties

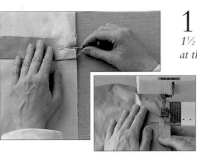

1 *Make two straight ties (see p.146), each measuring 1½ x 4in (4 x 25cm). Place one at the center of the right side at the top of the main panel. Place contrast flap right side down over the tie and pin in place. Machine stitch the contrast flap to main panel, stitching over the tie (see inset).*

2 *Press a ⅜in (1cm) double hem at each end of the cover and pin. Machine stitch in place. Pin the second tie to the center of the other end of the cover. Stitch around in a rectangle to attach the tie (see p.146). Fold the main panel in half so the base aligns with the seam of the top edge and contrast flap. Fold the contrast flap down over the main panel. Finish as in Step 2 of the envelope pillow.*

Envelope pillow with buttons

1 *Take the strip of contrast fabric measuring 3½ x 18in (9 x 45cm) and attach iron-on interfacing to the wrong side, following maker's instructions. Turn over a ⅜in (1cm) double hem along one side, pin, and stitch. Place the strip along one end of the main panel, right sides together, and pin. Machine stitch, making a ⅜in (1cm) seam allowance.*

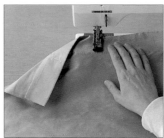

2 *Working from the right side of the cover with the interfaced strip underneath, mark the position of the buttonholes. Position one in the center and one 12.5in (5cm) each side of the center. Stitch the buttonholes by machine (see p.152).*

3 *Take a flap of contrast fabric 8 x 18in (20 x 45cm) and fold in half with wrong sides together. Stitch the folded fabric to the right side of the other end of the cover.*

4 *Fold the cover and stitch the side seams as in Step 2 of the envelope pillow. Turn the cover right side out and sew the buttons onto the contrast flap.*

MARBLED FIREPLACE

Creates a stunning focal point • Transforms a dull fireplace • Adds elegance

A MARBLED FIREPLACE adds an immediate touch of grandeur to a room. Although relatively easy and quick to do, marbling can look spectacular and effectively disguise a plain or ugly surround. In this simplified version of the technique, the whole area is painted with cream glaze and softened lightly with mutton cloth. Very fine lines are then added by hand to imitate veins of real marble. If you can, study some pieces of marble before you start work on your fireplace to help you create a convincing finish.

An elegant feature *With the help of the marbled finish, this fireplace becomes an elegant focal point in the room for a fraction of the cost of the real thing.*

PROJECT PLANNER

4 HOURS

Tools and Materials
Primer • White undercoat • White vinyl flat latex
• Cream vinyl flat latex • Raw umber artist's acrylic
• White artist's acrylic • Scumble glaze • Gloss polyurethane
varnish • Mutton cloth • Thin artist's brush
• Paintbrush • Softening brush • Brush for varnish

1 *If the fireplace is varnished or made of anything other than wood, apply a coat of primer. Make sure the surface is sanded and clean, and apply undercoat. Leave it to dry and apply one coat of white vinyl flat latex. Leave it to dry for 30 minutes.*

2 *Mix a glaze from cream vinyl flat latex, scumble glaze, and water (see p. 165). Apply one coat of glaze to the fireplace.*

3 *Take a piece of mutton cloth and tuck the edges in to make a neat pad. While the glaze is still damp, dab it with the mutton cloth to soften the brush marks and give some texture. Allow some areas to become slightly lighter than others.*

4 *Using a thin artist's brush and raw umber artist's acrylic, paint in some very fine diagonal lines to imitate the veins of real marble. Keep them irregular, twisting the brush as you go down. Do a few lines at a time; then soften them with a softening brush while they are still wet to make them more subtle (see inset).*

5 *With white artist's acrylic, add some white lines, twisting the brush as before to keep them irregular. Do a few lines at a time and soften while they are still wet as before. Keep the veins random – don't make a regular pattern.*

6 *When all the paint is dry, apply one coat of gloss polyurethane varnish to protect the fireplace.*

CUBE FOOTSTOOL

Versatile and practical • Inexpensive yet stylish • Quick to make

THIS UP-TO-DATE version of the footstool is simply a sleek foam cube, covered with a smooth-textured, suede-effect fabric. It doubles as a seat and occasional table, too. Use the firmest grade of upholstery foam available. If you cannot get the thickness required, ask your supplier to bond layers of foam together to the required depth. Two sizes are shown – a perfect cube and a slightly taller version. Check that the fabric you choose has been treated with Scotchgard™ or use a spray-on fabric protector to provide some protection from dirt and spills.

A minimalist shape *Select a strong, upholstery-grade fabric to cover the cube. Suede and leather-effect fabrics lend themselves to this minimalist shape, but corduroy and tweed would also look good.*

PROJECT PLANNER

2 HOURS

Tools and Materials

Foam cube measuring 16 x 16 x 16in (40 x 40 x 40cm) • Stockinette to cover (see p.155) • Piece of batting 16 x 16in (40 x 40cm) • Fabric: cut four panels for the sides, each 16 x 16in (40 x 40cm) plus ⅝in (1.5cm) seam allowance all around, plus two panels for the top and bottom, each 16 x 16in (40 x 40cm) plus ⅝in (1.5cm) seam allowance all around • Sewing machine and thread to match fabric

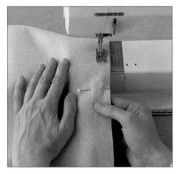

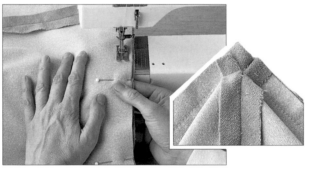

1 *Pin side panels, wrong sides together, making a ⅝in (1.5cm) seam allowance. Machine stitch.*

2 *Pin the top edges of all four side panels to the top panel, wrong sides together. Machine stitch. As you near a corner, clip the side panel seam to fit a round the corner (see p.136). At the corner, leave the needle in the work, lift foot, and pivot work. Lower the foot and continue stitching along top of next side panel (see inset).*

3 *When the stitching is complete, clip across each corner, taking care not to cut the stitching. This helps to reduce bulk and make the cover fit neatly over the cube.*

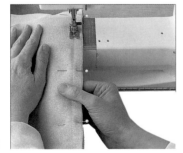

4 *Pin and machine stitch the base panel to the bottom of one side panel, making a ⅝in (1.5cm) seam allowance.*

5 *Press over a ⅝in (1.5cm) seam allowance on the remaining three sides of the base panel and on the free edges of the side panels.*

6 *Place the batting on top of the cube and cover the cube with stockinette (see p.155). Push the cube into the cover. Using a double length of thread, sew the open side with even slipstitch (see p.138).*

TROMPE L'OEIL PANELS

Simple yet striking • Adds interest to a plain expanse • Inexpensive to do

TROMPE L'OEIL tricks the eye into seeing a three-dimensional effect where there is only flat paint. These elegant, sophisticated panels are created by clever shading and are an excellent way of decorating a room without pictures. The effect is cool, clean, and harmonious and makes a room look bigger and more stylish. The centers of the panels are simply painted a darker shade than the rest of the wall and edged in a still darker tone and white to create the effect of shadow. The blue-gray here works well, but any closely related tones could be used.

Spacing for effect *Space your panels carefully for maximum effect. Too many can be overwhelming – here they work best used only above the dado level.*

PROJECT PLANNER

4 HOURS

Tools and Materials
Vinyl flat latex in three tones of blue-gray: light, medium, and dark • White vinyl flat latex • Paintbrush • 2in (5cm) paintbrush • Dragging brush • Low-tack masking tape • Pencil • Ruler • Level

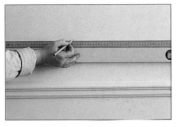

3 *Apply the medium gray vinyl flat latex within the masked panel. Using a dragging brush, drag the paint while still wet to get a subtle effect. Leave for 30 minutes or until touch dry.*

1 *Prepare the wall (see p.169) and paint it light gray (see p.166). Leave to dry. Measure and mark the panels above the dado rail (see p.177) using a ruler and level. The panels here measure 24 x 32in (60 x 80cm) with 12in (30cm) between each panel, but you can adapt these measurements to suit your wall.*

2 *Apply low-tack masking tape all around the outside edges of each panel.*

4 *Measure and mark 1in (2.5cm) in from the tape that marks the outside of the panel. Apply masking tape along the inside edges of this line as shown here.*

5 *At the bottom right of the panel, mark a line from corner to corner between the tapes. Place a piece of tape below that line. Tape the top left corner in the same way. Using a 2in (5cm) brush, apply white vinyl flat latex between the two pieces of tape on the top and right of the panel. Be sure to work right up to the tapes marking the corners (see inset). Leave to dry for 30 minutes.*

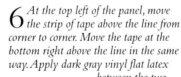

6 *At the top left of the panel, move the strip of tape above the line from corner to corner. Move the tape at the bottom right above the line in the same way. Apply dark gray vinyl flat latex between the two pieces of tape at the bottom and left of the panel, working right up to the corner tapes as before (see inset).*

7 *The finished panel should have dark gray on the left and bottom, and white on the right and top to create the shadow lines that give the 3D effect. Remove tape. Repeat Steps 2 to 6 to complete the remaining panels.*

THROW

Coordinates your color scheme • Adds texture and variation • Warm and cozy

A THROW IS AN extremely useful decorating device – a clever choice of fabric or color can help tie together disparate elements of a decorating scheme. Use a throw to introduce a touch of contrast color to enliven a monochrome scheme or add an element of soft and contrasting texture to a hard-surfaced room. By finishing the throw with lavish trimmings, you can create instant style and luxury. But, don't forget that on a chilly evening, a throw's primary function is to provide extra warmth and comfort. The throw shown here is made with two layers of soft and textured chenille in up-to-the-minute colors, trimmed with a chunky bullion fringe.

Draping fabrics *Choose fabrics that drape beautifully and feel good to the touch. Don't forget to look at dress fabrics as well, but avoid fabrics that crease easily such as linen or crisp cotton.*

PROJECT PLANNER

2½ HOURS

Tools and Materials
For a throw measuring 4 x 5ft (1.2 x 1.5m), cut two pieces of fabric this size, plus ¾in (2cm) seam allowances • 2¾yd (2.5m) fringe • Masking tape • Sewing machine and thread to match fabric

1 *Cut the length of fringe in half – one half for each short side of the fabric. Put a piece of masking tape at each end of the fringe to stop it from fraying. Place one piece of fabric right side up and pin a length of fringe to each short side. Baste (see p. 138) it in place.*

2 *Place the other panel of fabric right side down on top of fringed fabric. Baste all around, leaving a large opening at the center of one long side. Take care to stitch at the base of the fringe welt and to stitch through all layers. At the corners, stitch between the fringe tassels.*

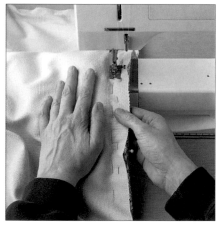

3 *Machine stitch all a round, except for the opening, following the line of basting and making sure you stitch through all layers. At the corners take a couple of stitches across the corner before pivoting the fabric and stitching down the next side (see blunting corners p. 136).*

4 *Cut across each corner of the throw, trimming off the protruding tassels.*

5 *Remove the basting stitches and turn the throw right side out. Tuck in the raw edges at the opening and pin. Handsew the folded edges together using even slipstitch (see p. 138).*

DECOUPAGE SCREEN

Stylish room divide • Popular decorative technique • Can be themed for your room

DECOUPAGE IS a traditional way of decorating items such as screens, trays, and small pieces of furniture. In Victorian times, découpage usually involved large numbers of small pictures carefully cut out and overlapped to cover the item completely. A more modern approach to the technique is to use larger, bolder items and place them more sparingly.

A simple screen makes a useful way of dividing a room or concealing clutter and can be designed to compliment the theme of the rest of the decor. This screen is given an oriental look, with the images of beautiful blue and white ceramics, but the possibilities are endless. The quality of color photocopies is now excellent, and the pictures used here have also been enlarged for maximum impact.

A modern look

Big, bold pictures will give your découpage a more contemporary look. Always be sure to plan the whole design on the floor before starting.

PROJECT PLANNER

Tools and Materials

Pictures or color photocopies • Vinyl flat latex in chosen base color • Gloss varnish • White glue • Paintbrush • Soft brush for varnishing • Small, sharp scissors • Waterproof abrasive paper • Soft cloth

15 HOURS

1 *Choose your images and make color photocopies, enlarging them if necessary. Simple shapes are best. Cut the images out very carefully, using small, sharp scissors.*

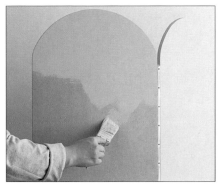

2 *Apply a coat of vinyl flat latex over both sides of the screen and let the paint dry for 30 minutes.*

3 *Plan your design. Apply glue to the back of the image that is to go at the top of the screen. Make sure the whole area is covered with an even coat of glue.*

4 *Place the glued image lightly on the screen and smooth it with a piece of cloth or dishtowel to even out any bumps. Make sure it is perfectly flat and in place. Any stubborn lumps will disappear as the glue dries.*

5 *Glue the next image in position as before. Attach the remaining images the same way, making sure each one is well glued and smooth.*

6 *When everything is positioned, leave the screen to dry overnight. The next day, apply a coat of varnish over the whole screen, including the découpage images. Use a very soft paintbrush so you don't get too many brushmarks.*

7 *Use waterproof abrasive paper to sand the screen, working very lightly over the images. Repeat Steps 6 and 7 until you have about five coats of varnish, leaving each coat to dry for about 30 minutes. This will give a durable, high-gloss finish to your screen.*

ROMAN SHADE

A simplified version • Neat and economical • Easy to hang

A ROMAN SHADE makes economical use of fabric and space, and is a useful covering for windows with little room at either side for curtains. This simplified version has only one rod and rod casing, and is rather less tailored and severe than the normal design. Fabrics should be lightweight and soft rather than crisp – linen, voile, or thin cotton are all suitable. The shade is attached with touch-and-close tape to a covered batten. The batten can be screwed into the recess of the window, or attached to the window frame or the wall above with right-angle brackets.

A simple look *Emphasize the shade's simplicity by choosing a plain fabric or graphic patterns, such as stripes, checks, or a single repeating motif that will not be lost when the shade is raised.*

PROJECT PLANNER

Tools and Materials

Main fabric: finished length plus 9in (23cm) hem allowances x finished width plus 4in (10cm) side seam allowances; (see p.129 for information on measuring window) • Lining: finished length, less 6in (15cm), plus ¾in (2cm) seam allowances x finished width, less 1½in (4cm) • Touch-and-close tape to fit finished width • Dowel to fit finished width • Rings for cording the back of the shade (see p.145) • Tailor's chalk • Sewing machine and thread to match fabric

3 HOURS

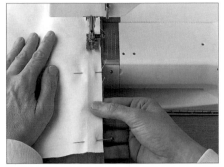

1 *Place main fabric and lining right sides together, aligning top edges. Pin and machine stitch side seams, making a ⅝in (1.5cm) seam allowance.*

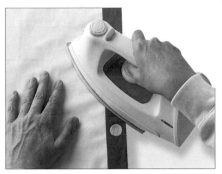

2 *Turn right side out and center the lining so it is about 1½in (3.5cm) in from each side. Press along each side.*

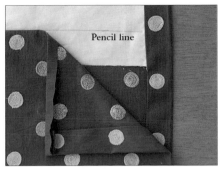

Pencil line

3 *Draw a pencil line across the bottom of the lining 2in (5cm) up from the bottom edge. Turn a ⅜in (1cm) hem up along bottom of main fabric and press. Fold main fabric up to meet the pencil line. Press and pin in place.*

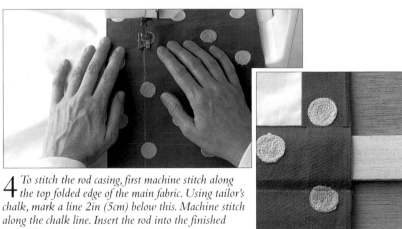

4 *To stitch the rod casing, first machine stitch along the top folded edge of the main fabric. Using tailor's chalk, mark a line 2in (5cm) below this. Machine stitch along the chalk line. Insert the rod into the finished casing (see inset).*

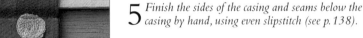

5 *Finish the sides of the casing and seams below the casing by hand, using even slipstitch (see p.138).*

6 *Fold over ¾in (2cm) at top edge of shade. Pin and press. Attach the touch-and-close strip (soft side), machine stitching at the top and bottom of the strip.*

7 *Attach the rings for cording the shade. Using couching stitch (see p.139) sew one ring 4in (10cm) in from the edge of the shade at the top of the casing. Stitch another in the center and a third 4in (10cm) from the other side of the shade. Stitch the next row 8in (20cm) above the first (see p.145 for more information on cording). Make sure you attach the rings through all layers of fabric. Attach the shade to a covered lath (see p.144).*

CRACKLE FRAMES

Unites assorted frames • Coordinates with pictures • Makes dull frames special

CRACKLE GLAZE simulates the effect of old paint that has cracked and peeled slightly to reveal another layer underneath. It can be used to rejuvenate a battered old frame or make a cheap wooden frame into something special. Crackle glaze also helps coordinate a group of different frames and give them a pleasingly aged look. Choose colors that work with your room or with the pictures to be framed. The technique is very simple. Two different colors of vinyl latex are used. A coat of crackle glaze is applied over the first coat of paint and left to dry. When the second color is applied, the glaze causes it to crack slightly as it dries, revealing the first color beneath. Crackle glaze could also be used on other small items such as boxes and lamp bases.

Pleasing harmony
A collection of frames is given a pleasing harmony with crackle glaze. If you are working on several items, try changing the order in which you apply the two colors for a varied yet coordinated effect.

PROJECT PLANNER

5 3/4 HOURS

Tools and Materials
Two contrasting colors of vinyl flat latex • Crackle glaze
•Varnish (flat, satin or gloss) • Paintbrushes • Brush for
varnishing • Sandpaper

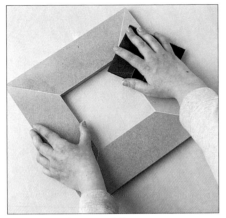

1 *Sand the frame carefully, removing any rough or uneven areas.*

2 *Apply a coat of one color of vinyl latex to the frame. Let it dry for about 30 minutes.*

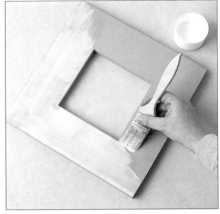

3 *Apply crackle glaze to the frame. Work around the frame in one direction and make sure the whole area is covered. Leave the glaze to dry for three hours.*

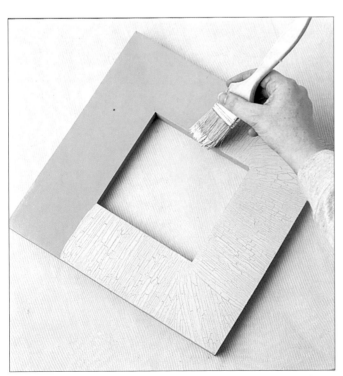

4 *Apply one coat of the second color of vinyl latex, working across the frame at right angles to the direction of the glaze. Leave this coat to dry for an hour or until touch dry.*

5 *Add a coat of varnish — flat, satin or gloss depending on how much shine you want. Apply the varnish in the same direction as the second coat of paint (Step 4).*

PLEATED DRAPES WITH VALANCE

Simple but unusual design • Integral valance • Sheers and heavier fabrics

THE APPEAL OF these drapes lies in the horizontal pleats at the base and on the self-valance, which provide textural interest and shape. Ties made from bias-cut strips of the same fabric are inserted into the seam between the valance and the drapes, and then tied over the pole to hold the drapes in place. The style is perfect for sheer dress drapes that are always drawn, but these drapes can be difficult to open and close. If you need to open the drapes frequently, it may be best to tie them to drape rings rather than directly onto the pole.

Choosing fabric *Select solid fabrics that speak for themselves, such as natural linen and fine cotton or the raw silk used here. This style would also suit sheer fabrics such as crisp voile or organza.*

PROJECT PLANNER

7 HOURS

Tools and Materials

Draperies: cut two, each measuring the finished drop, plus 1½in (4cm) seam allowances, plus 12½in (32cm) for pleats x 1½ times the width of window (see p.128) • Valance: cut two, each measuring 12in (30cm), plus 1½in (4cm) seam allowances, plus 6¼in (12½in) for pleats x 1½ times the width of window (see p.128) • Ties: 12 bias-cut ties (see p.148) with a finished width of 1in (2.5cm) and length of 20in (50cm) • Tailor's chalk • Sewing machine and thread to match fabric

1 *Fold in a ¾in (2cm) double hem along the base and sides of each drape. Pin, press, and machine stitch.*

2 *Using tailor's chalk and working on the right side of the drape, draw a line across the drape 4in (10cm) from the base. Draw another line 4¾in (12cm) above that, then two more at 4¾in (12cm) intervals.*

3 *Starting at top chalk line, press drape over at each line, wrong sides together. Pin in place to form pleats.*

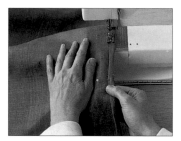

4 *Machine stitch each pleat 1½in (4cm) above the fold line to hold it in place. To help keep your stitching straight, stick a piece of masking tape on the machine as a guide (see p.135). To make the valance, repeat Steps 1 to 4 with the valance fabric, but marking only two lines, one 4in (10cm) from the base and one 4¾in (12cm) above that.*

5 *Make six bias ties for each drape (see p.148). Fold each tie in half and pin the folded edge to the top of the wrong side of the drape. Place one just in from each side and space the rest evenly across the width. (If your drape is very wide, you may need more than six ties.) With the right side of the valance face down, pin it to the top edge of the wrong side of the drape (see inset).*

6 *Machine stitch the valance to the top of the drape, stitching across the ties. Press the seam open and flip the valance to the right side of the drape. Tie onto the drape pole.*

DINING ROOMS

TABLE NAPKINS AND PLACEMATS

Creates a coordinated look • Simple to make • Protect your table

PLACEMATS WITH matching napkins create a pretty table setting, especially when they are made with fabric as appetizing as this pretty strawberry print. The design came in a choice of fabrics – a heavy linen that was ideal for the placemats and a crisp cotton that suited the napkins. Whatever fabric you choose will have to survive repeated laundering, so make sure it is preshrunk and colorfast. The placemats, which are lined with plain linen for added durability, are edged with narrow red bias binding to highlight the reds and pinks in the print. The edges of the napkins are simply folded over and oversewn with a row of machine satin stitching in vibrant red thread. Either of these finishes could be used for both placemats and napkins. Your choice will depend on the fabric you have chosen, your equipment – does your machine sew satin stitch smoothly, for example – and your personal taste.

An alternative finish
Here the edges of the fabric have been neatly frayed to create an attractive fringed effect.

PROJECT PLANNER

Tools and Materials

Main fabric for four placemats: each measures 12 x 16in (30 x 40cm) including seam allowances
• Lining for four placemats: as main fabric • Bias binding: allow 1¾yd (1.5m) of ½in (12mm)
binding for each mat • Fabric for four napkins: each measures 16½ x 16½in (42 x 42cm),
including seam allowances • Sewing machine and thread to match or contrast with fabric
(napkins need contrasting thread)

Placemats

1 *Pin main fabric and lining wrong sides together. Machine stitch, leaving seam allowance of ½in (12mm). Very carefully, trim seam allowance close to the line of stitching (see inset).*

2 *Open the bias binding. Pin to one end of the mat, aligning edges. Machine stitch on the right of the first fold. Turn the binding to the other side, pin, and topstitch by machine, (working from the right side). Trim flush with end of fabric. Repeat at the other end. Stitch binding to a long side of the mat, leaving ½in (12mm) over at each end.*

3 *Turn the bias binding to the wrong side of the mat, pin in place, and topstitch. When you reach the corners, turn the ends of the binding in and stitch over them, backstitching to secure (see inset). Repeat on the other long side of the mat.*

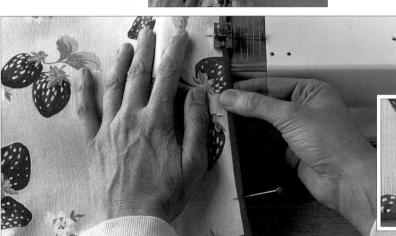

Napkin

1 *Turn in a ½in (12mm) seam allowance all around the napkin, mitering corners (see p.137) and press. Machine stitch on wrong side, keeping very close to the raw edges. Use the contrasting thread to make a clear line to follow when working satin stitch.*

2 *Turn to the right side and stitch all around with narrow machine satin stitch (see p.135). Follow the previous line of stitching, keeping it in the center of the satin stitch. At the corners, leave the needle in the work, lift the foot, and turn the work. Lower the foot and continue stitching in the new direction (see p.135).*

STAMPED WALLS

Simple wallpaper effect • Create your own design • Simple to do

Tʜɪs sɪᴍᴘʟᴇ ᴛᴇᴄʜɴɪQᴜᴇ allows you to create the decorative look of wallpaper without the trouble. A wide selection of wooden stamps is available that you can use to create your own individual design. The wall is first painted in your chosen base color. Once you have measured the wall and worked out your design, mark the position of each stamp. Then you simply apply paint to the

stamp and stamp the wall. Try to keep the stamps reasonably even, although a slight variation in density will add to the charm of this technique.

Simple shapes *Simple graphic shapes work best for this stamping technique. Keep them well spaced – if the shapes are too close together, the wall will look too busy.*

PROJECT PLANNER

3 HOURS

Tools and Materials
Vinyl flat latex in two shades: one light, one dark • Wooden stamp • Small and large paintbrushes • Ruler • Pencil • Carpenter's level

1 *Prepare the wall (see p. 169) and apply undercoat if necessary. Apply the lighter of your two shades of vinyl latex with a brush or roller (see p. 166). Leave it to dry.*

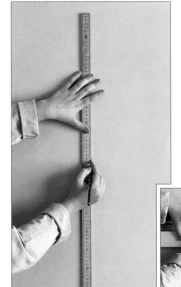

2 *Measure the wall and mark dots to help you position the stamp (see p. 177). Each dot should mark the bottom left-hand corner of the stamp. The stamp here measures 4 x 4in (10 x 10cm) and there is 16in (40cm) between each stamp and 24in (60cm) between each horizontal row. Alternate rows should be staggered as shown. Use a level to check your lines of dots are straight (see inset).*

3 *Take the darker shade of vinyl latex and apply it to the stamp with a small brush. Make sure the design is covered evenly and completely. There should be no lumps of excess paint on the stamp.*

4 *Place the stamp on the wall, aligning the bottom left-hand corner with the dot. Roll the stamp forward, pressing hard to lay the paint – the curved base allows it to be rocked. Lift the stamp off the wall with one clean movement. It is a good idea to practice stamping on a piece of paper before starting on the wall.*

5 *Continue stamping until the wall is complete, reapplying paint each time to get stamps of a reasonably even density.*

REVERSIBLE TABLECLOTH

Two cloths in one • Protects your table • Adaptable and versatile

W HEN CHOOSING textile accessories for a dining room, it is important to strike the right balance between style and practicality. While a tablecloth helps make the room look attractive, it also has to protect polished wood surfaces from hot dishes and occasional spills as well as from daily wear and tear. Whether the effect you wish to create is chic and formal or comfortable and cozy, fabrics for table covers need to be easy to care for and durable. A reversible tablecloth is decorative and extremely practical. Combine coordinating but distinctly different

fabrics with a border that is complimentary to both, and you will be able to make changes as occasion or mood demands by simply flipping the cloth over. Perhaps one side could be used for family meals and the other for more formal dining.

The amount of overhang on the cloth can be adapted to your taste and the look of your table (see p.131). Check that the fabrics you choose have been preshrunk and are colorfast. If you are uncertain, wash all three fabrics before you start to make the cloth.

Two looks
Bold stripes and flowers on one side and a geometric pattern on the other (see inset) give this cloth two completely different looks. The sunny blue border complements both fabrics and provides a harmonizing note.

PROJECT PLANNER

Tools and Materials

Main fabric: two pieces the length and width of your table, plus overhang (see p.131), less the finished border depth; add ½in (12mm) seam allowance all around • Border fabric to make a border with a finished depth of 3in (7.5cm): two strips the length of the long sides of the main fabric x 7in (18cm); two strips the length of the short sides of the main fabric, plus 6in (15cm), plus 1in (2.5cm) for seam allowances x 7in (18cm) • Sewing machine and thread to match fabric

1 Place the two pieces of main fabric wrong sides together. Pin, making sure they are lying perfectly flat and that all the edges are neatly aligned. Handsew around all four sides ½in (12mm) in from the edges, using large basting stitches (see p.138).

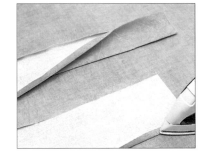

2 Press a ½in (12mm) seam allowance on both long sides of one of the borders. Fold the border in half and press again so the folded edges are aligned. Repeat with the remaining borders. The width of the fabric shown here is 7in (18cm) to make a border of 3in (7.5cm).

3 Take a long border, open out the folds, and place it along one of the long sides of the cloth, right sides together. Pin the border in place along the pressed fold line marking the seam allowance, making sure each end of the border is aligned with the edge of the cloth. Machine stitch along the fold.

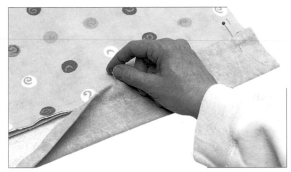

4 Turn the cloth over and pin the border to the other side of the cloth so the folded edge meets the line of machine stitching.

5 Turn the cloth back to the top side. Machine stitch the border close to the fold line, making sure the stitching also catches the border on the other side. Attach the second long border the same way.

6 Take a short border and place it right side down along one of the short sides of the cloth. The end of the border should project ½in (12mm) beyond the edge of the cloth for finishing later. Pin in place and machine stitch.

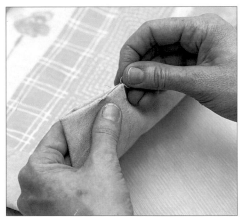

7 Turn and finish as for the long borders Step 3, but tuck in the ends as you fold the border over. Handsew the folded ends together, using uneven slipstitch (see p.138). Repeat Steps 6 and 7 to attach the remaining border. Remove any basting that is still visible.

FAUX LACQUER CABINET

Classic Eastern style • Suits furniture with clean lines

A PLAIN WOODEN cabinet can be transformed into a spectacular piece of furniture with this faux lacquer technique. The project may seem lengthy, but much of this is drying time and the method is not complicated. The item is painted with several coats of red paint, sanding between each coat to achieve as smooth a finish as possible. A watery coat of raw umber and a spattering of white and

black dots simulates something of the depth of the real thing. Finally, three coats of varnish are applied to achieve a high-gloss finish.

Oriental style *Several layers of gleaming red paint and glossy varnish turn an ordinary wooden cabinet into an item of Eastern style and beauty.*

PROJECT PLANNER

5½ HOURS

Tools and Materials

White vinyl flat latex • Red vinyl flat latex • Artist's acrylic paint in raw umber, black, and white • Gloss acrylic varnish • Paintbrushes • Small stippling brush for flicking • Softening brush • Soft brush for varnish • Waterproof abrasive paper

1 *Prepare the item to be lacquered (see p. 168). Sand to remove any rough areas. Apply one coat of white vinyl latex. Leave it to dry for at least 30 minutes.*

2 *Apply the first coat of red vinyl latex to the item and leave it to dry thoroughly – for at least an hour.*

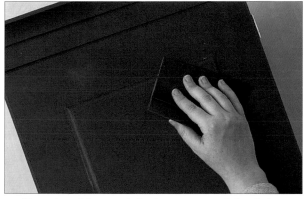

3 *Use a piece of dampened abrasive paper to sand the whole item. Apply two more coats of red paint, sanding between each coat with damp abrasive paper. Apply the paint in different directions each time to avoid getting a build-up in any particular area. The finish should be as smooth as possible with no visible brush marks.*

4 *Mix a small amount of raw umber artist's acrylic paint with water. The consistency should be very watery so the paint appears almost translucent when applied. Apply one thin coat over the whole item and soften with a softening brush while still wet.*

5 *Mix a small amount of black artist's acrylic paint with water to a watery consistency. Dip a small stippling brush into the paint and, using your thumb, flick small dots of paint over the item. Don't have too much paint on the brush – the dots should be subtle and not too close together. (Practice this technique on a piece of newspaper before trying it on the lacquered item.) Repeat with white paint, again keeping the dots very subtle (see inset). There should be fewer white dots than black.*

6 *Let the paint dry thoroughly. Using gloss varnish and a soft brush, apply three coats of varnish, sanding with waterproof abrasive paper between each coat. Leave each coat of varnish for 30 minutes or until touch dry before applying the next one. If you do not want a high-gloss finish, use satin varnish for the last coat.*

TIE-ON SEAT CUSHIONS

Make hard chairs comfortable • Easy to wash • Made to fit individual chairs

SOFTEN THE LOOK of wooden or metal dining chairs with tailored tie-on squab cushions. These will not only provide comfort, but also allow you to use fabric and color to coordinate with other elements in the room.

To make sure the cushion fits the seat exactly, make a template of the shape of the seat out of newspaper and ask a foam supplier to cut the required number of cushions from 1in (2.5cm) deep fire-retardant foam. Soften the shape of the foam by covering it snugly with a layer of batting and lining before covering. Measure the finished lined shape and make another template from which to cut your fabric. Place the cut fabric shape on the chair and mark the position of the ties in relation to the struts on the chair. There is no need for a zipper in the back of these cushions – they are small enough to put in the washing machine, but make sure the fabric is washable.

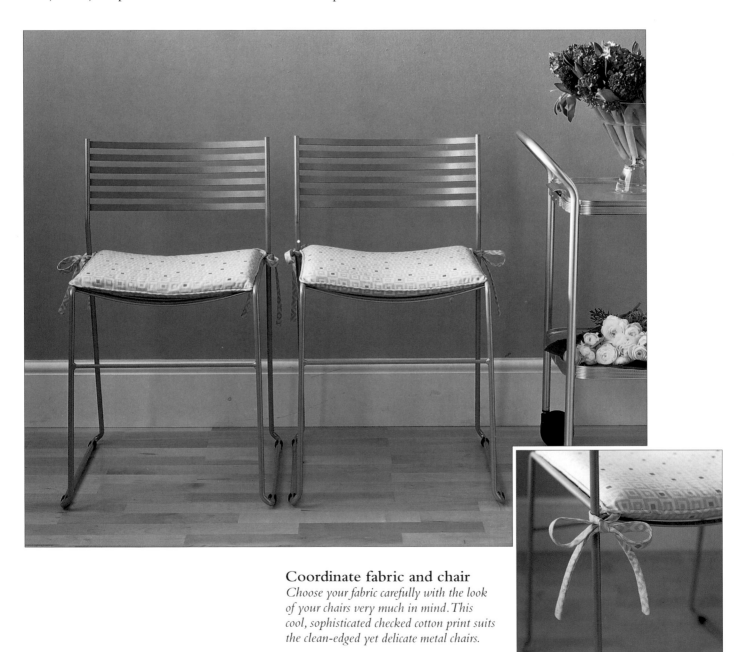

Coordinate fabric and chair
Choose your fabric carefully with the look of your chairs very much in mind. This cool, sophisticated checked cotton print suits the clean-edged yet delicate metal chairs.

PROJECT PLANNER

4 HOURS

Tools and Materials

For two cushions: two foam pads cut to fit chair seats • Fabric (see p.131 for how to measure): cut two panels for each cushion the size of the foam pad plus ⅝in (1.5cm) seam allowance all around • Fabric for bias piping and ties • Piping cord • Sewing machine and thread to match fabric

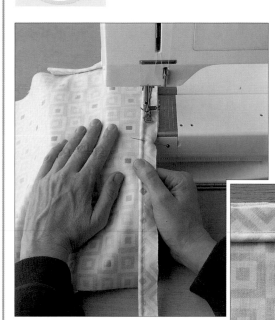

1 *Make piping (see p.150) to fit all around the cushion. Pin and machine stitch to the right side of the top panel of fabric, with a seam allowance of ⅝in (1.5cm). At the corners, snip into the seam allowance of the piping (see p.151) so it fits neatly (see inset).*

2 *Make four bias-cut ties (see p.148). For a chair with corner struts, pin the ties on each side of the two back corners of the top panel as shown. If the struts of your chair are farther in, you could place the ties one on top of the other. Handsew the ties in place.*

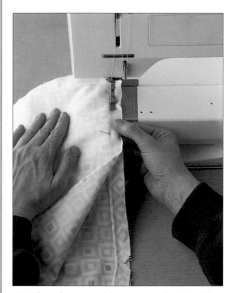

3 *Place the top and bottom panels right sides together and pin. Machine stitch around three sides, leaving the back open. Stitch with the left-hand edge of the foot along the ridge of the piping underneath. Stitch carefully over ties at corners or wherever they are positioned so they are held between the two layers of fabric.*

4 *To reduce bulk at the corners, trim off each corner and then trim a little more fabric from each side of the corner.*

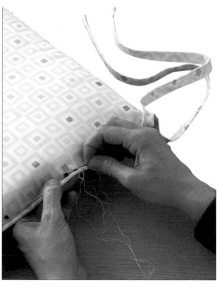

5 *Turn the cover right side out and press. Press the seam allowance of ⅝in (1.5cm) on the unstitched edge. Put the foam panel into the cover and handsew the open side closed with slipstitch (see p.138).*

COLORWASH WALLS

Quick and easy • Adds texture to walls • Disguises rough walls

A RELAXED, INFORMAL effect, colorwashing brings some movement and texture to paintwork – a change from flat, even color. It is also an excellent way of concealing uneven plastering. The wall is first painted with cream latex. The glaze is then added in sections, using large, crisscrossing strokes, and brushed out with a dry badger brush while still wet. A ready-mixed colorwash can be used, or you can make your own, using scumble glaze and your own combination of artist's acrylic colors (see p.165).

Timeless beauty *Warm and vibrant, a terra-cotta colorwash is an ideal background for minimalist furniture. The technique gives a feeling of age and timeless beauty to any interior.*

PROJECT PLANNER

1¾ HOURS

Tools and Materials
Cream vinyl flat latex • Terra-cotta colorwash (ready-mixed or see p.165 for instructions on mixing your own glaze) • Paint bucket • Paintbrush • Badger brush

1 *Prepare the wall (see p.169) and apply a coat of cream vinyl latex. The yellower the color of the base coat, the warmer the final colorwash will be. Leave it to dry.*

2 *Apply the colorwash in sections (see p.170), using large, crisscrossing strokes (see p.167). Take the brush down from the right to the left and then from the left, down to the right with a flowing motion.*

3 *With a dry badger brush and while the glaze is still wet, soften the strokes on the area you have painted. Use crisscrossing strokes again, brushing first one way and then the other.*

4 *Apply colorwash to the next section as quickly as possible before the wet edge dries. Make sure this is carefully blended with the one before, leaving no white areas or hard lines.*

5 *Continue colorwashing and softening until the wall is covered. Pay particular attention to the seams between sections.*

TORTOISESHELL LAMP BASE

Rejuvenates an old lamp • Gives a sophisticated look • Simple to achieve

A TORTOISESHELL FINISH is not difficult to achieve and can be used to transform small items such as lamp bases, boxes, and trays. As with all faux effects, study the real thing if you can before starting so you know the look you are aiming for.

The item is painted with warm yellow paint and then given a coat of wood stain. The side of a brush is used to make zigzag marks in the stain, and some irregular lines are added in artist's acrylic paint. These are softened with a dry brush, and the item is varnished to high-gloss finish.

A luxurious look *Make an old wooden lamp base into something special with a luxurious tortoiseshell effect. Several different bases could be coordinated using this technique.*

PROJECT PLANNER

Tools and Materials

11 HOURS

Oil-based warm yellow paint • Mahogany wood stain • Raw umber artist's oil paint • Black artist's oil paint • Turpentine • Gloss varnish • Paintbrushes • Small artist's brush • Softening brush • Soft brush for varnishing

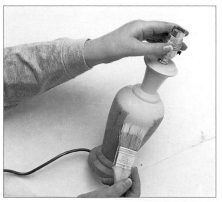

1 *If the lamp base is plain wood, you can paint straight onto it. If it already has a coat of paint, sand this before starting. Apply a coat of oil-based warm yellow paint all over the lamp base and leave it to dry for one hour.*

2 *Apply a coat of mahogany wood stain over the whole lamp base.*

3 *While the stain is wet and using the side of the brush, make zigzag shapes in the stain all over the lamp base.*

4 *Using a little dark brown artist's oil paint and a small brush, add some small irregular lines over the surface.*

5 *Clean the brush with turpentine and repeat Step 4 with black oil paint, but make fewer, smaller lines and leave more space between them.*

6 *Take a clean, dry softening brush and lightly stroke it back and forth across the black and brown lines while they are still wet to soften them. Leave the lamp base to dry overnight.*

7 *Using gloss varnish and a soft brush, apply a coat of varnish to the lamp base and leave to dry thoroughly.*

GATHERED VALANCE

Creates drama and atmosphere • Unusual design • Gives old draperies a new look

A VALANCE can make a dramatic statement over plain curtains and helps to give an illusion of height to a small window. Simple to make, the valance is gathered to its finished width and a strip of velcro is sewn over the gathers. It is then attached to a shelf that is mounted at the top of the window frame with right-angle shelf brackets. If there is room, the valance can be positioned above the window. When working out the width of the valance, remember that it must extend around the sides of the valance shelf (the returns) as well as across the front.

Contrasting stripes *Strips of black and cream fabric have been sewn together to make wide stripes and then finished with a shaped hem to create a softly gathered valance.*

PROJECT PLANNER

2½ HOURS

Tools and Materials

Fabric: panels of contrasting fabric, each panel measuring 7in (18cm) (including 1¼in [3cm] seam allowances) x 27in (68cm), to make a joined valance two and a half times the width of the valance shelf and returns • Lining fabric to fit joined panels, and an extra strip the finished width of the valance x 2¼in (5.5cm) • 1in (2.5cm) curtain heading tape • Touch-and-close tape to fit finished width of valance • Cardboard • Tailor's chalk • Sewing machine and thread to match fabric

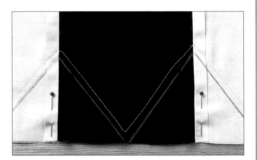

1 *Pin and machine stitch panels wrong sides together, making ⅝in (1.5cm) seam allowances, to make the required width of the valance. Press the seams open.*

2 *Copy the template on p.179 onto a piece of cardboard. Place the template on the wrong side of the fabric so the points touch the bottom edge. Draw around the template with tailor's chalk. Lay the joined panels on the lining and pin, right sides together.*

3 *Machine stitch panels and lining together, keeping the right-hand edge of the foot on the line. At a point, stop, lift the foot, and pivot the work. Take one stitch across the point, lift the foot again, and turn to go up the other side of the point.*

4 *Using a pair of sharp scissors, cut around the stitched shape, keeping about ¼in (5mm) away from the stitching. Clip off the ends of points (see inset).*

5 *Turn the valance right side out. Using a pencil held inside the fabric, gently tease out the tip of each point. Press the valance carefully.*

6 *At the top of the valance, turn over 3in (7.5cm) to the lining side and press. Using tailor's chalk, mark a line 2½in (6cm) from the top. Pin the curtain tape in place with the top on the line. Machine stitch top and bottom (see p.141).*

7 *Pull up the cords on the tape to gather the valance to the required width. Tie and finish the cords neatly (see p.141). Attach touch-and-close (soft side) to the lining fabric and stitch to the valance (see p.142). Prepare the shelf (see p.142), ready to hang your valance.*

Kitchens

BENCH CUSHION

Comfortable and practical • Quick to make • Adds color to your kitchen

THIS SIMPLE BOX cushion is ideal for use on a bench or window seat. Instead of having a separate box strip and piping, the cover is cut in one piece and sewn together like a flat cushion cover. Each corner is then squared off with a mitered seam.

To make a change, combine two coordinating fabrics and make another slipcover to tie over the first. This is a practical as well as attractive solution in a busy family kitchen – in the event of spills, you can remove the outer slipcover to wash, while leaving the main cover in place. The cushions used here have been made to measure, using soft, manmade filling, which gives a rounded shape and is machine washable. You could, however, use this type of cover on a foam pad for a more defined and boxy shape and a firmer seat. Such cushions are likely to get heavy wear, especially in a kitchen, so choose sturdy, durable fabric.

Perfect partners *Stripes and checks make perfect partners for these coordinating cushion covers. The outer cushion is tied on with lengths of ordinary tape or ribbon.*

PROJECT PLANNER

2 HOURS

Tools and Materials

Foam pad or cushion to fit your bench • Fabric for outer sleeve: the length of the cushion plus the depth plus 1¼in (3cm) x twice the width plus the depth plus 1¼in (3cm) • Fabric for inner sleeve: length of the cushion plus the depth plus 1¼in (3cm) x twice the width plus twice the depth plus 1¼in (3cm) • 1⅜yd (1.2m) of ribbon or tape for ties • Zipper measuring three quarters of cushion length • Sewing machine and thread to match fabric

Inner sleeve

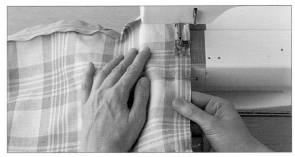

1 *Fold the inner sleeve fabric in half lengthwise, right sides together. Mark length of zipper with pins. Machine stitch down to zipper, making a ⅝in (1.5cm) seam allowance, and backstitch to secure. Stitch below zipper. Insert the zipper (see p.153).*

2 *Machine stitch side seams of the inner sleeve, making a ⅝in (1.5cm) seam allowance.*

3 *Press side seams flat. Machine stitch across the corners at the point where the line of stitching is the same as the depth of the cushion to make the box shape (see p.137). Trim off excess fabric at the corner (see inset).*

Outer sleeve

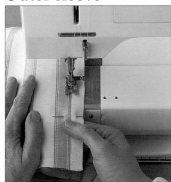

4 *Fold fabric in half and pin and stitch side seams, making a ⅝in (1.5cm) seam allowance. Box corners as in Step 3 (see p.137).*

5 *Press under a ⅜in (1cm) double hem to the wrong side all around the open edge and pin. Machine stitch close to the bottom edge and then machine stitch close to the top edge.*

6 *Cut four ties each measuring about 12in (30cm). Position one tie about one-third of the way from one end and the other one-third from the other end on the top of the cover. Pin the other two ties in the same position on the bottom of the cushion. To attach securely, turn under the raw end of the tie. Stitch around the end of the tie in a box shape and then stitch diagonally across (see p.146).*

DRAGGED CABINET DOORS

Gives a new look to old cabinet • Inexpensive • Classic Shaker style

GIVE THE DOORS of old kitchen units a sophisticated Shaker-style look with this simple dragging technique. You may be bored with your old units or have inherited some that are perfectly sound but simply not to your taste – this finish will cover a multitude of sins.

The doors are first covered with a coat of shellac-based primer. This can be used on any surface and provides a good surface to paint over. Take care when using this primer and always be sure to keep the room well ventilated while working. The primer ruins paintbrushes, too, so use an old one that can be thrown away afterward. Once the primer is dry, two coats of white latex are applied. Finally, the door is given a coat of cream glaze and dragged to give a subtle yet textured finish. A coat of strong polyurethane varnish will protect the finished dragged doors from normal kitchen wear and tear.

New look
Battered old doors or ugly new ones can be transformed by this sleek, modern finish. Drag downward on the center panels and vertical stiles and across on the horizontal stiles.

PROJECT PLANNER

Tools and Materials

Shellac-based primer • White vinyl flat latex • Cream vinyl flat latex • Scumble glaze • Old brush for primer • Paintbrushes • Dragging brush • Strong polyurethane varnish in satin or gloss • Sandpaper

3 HOURS

1 *Make sure the doors are clean and dry and free of any wax or oil. Sand the doors to remove any uneven areas and make a smooth surface to give a fine finish.*

2 *Using an old brush, apply one coat of shellac-based primer. Let it dry for about 30 minutes. This primer can be used over anything and gives a surface to work on without having to strip what is there. Make sure the area is well ventilated when using primer.*

3 *Apply two coats of white vinyl latex to the doors. Let each coat of paint stand until dry to the touch – about 30 minutes.*

4 *Mix a glaze from cream vinyl latex, scumble glaze, and water (see p.165). Apply to the door a section at a time and drag while still wet. Take the dragging brush down from top to bottom in straight strokes. At the base, sweep the brush up slightly so the paint doesn't collect. For horizontal stiles, drag the brush across.*

5 *Apply one coat of strong polyurethane satin varnish, or use gloss for a high shine. Brush the varnish in the same direction as the paint – vertically on the main part of the doors and across on the horizontal stiles.*

CHECKED WALLS

Fresh, bright look • Quick and simple • Practical

THESE CHEERFUL checks give the look of wallpaper, but are much more practical in the hot, steamy atmosphere of a kitchen. Extremely simple to achieve, each pair of thick and thin stripes is produced with one stroke of a specially cut foam roller. First the vertical stripes are applied and then the horizontal, working as smoothly as possible and keeping the roller as straight as you can. If you do need to stop in mid-stripe to put more paint on the roller, roll up the stripe slightly before stopping so that you don't get a telltale line.

Kitchen checks *Fresh and vibrant, these bright green checks make a perfect wall covering for a friendly family kitchen. For advice on working around doors and windows, see p. 176.*

PROJECT PLANNER

3 HOURS

Tools and Materials
White vinyl flat latex • Vinyl flat latex in chosen color • Mini-roller, usually 4¼in (11cm) wide • Paint tray • Masking tape • Utility knife • Pencil • Ruler • Cutting board

1 *Prepare the wall (see p. 169) and apply a base coat of white vinyl latex (see p. 166). This will be the background to the checks. Leave the wall to dry for 30 minutes.*

2 *Take the mini-roller, mark a section 1¼in (3cm) from one end and cut out the foam (see p. 174). This will give you one thick stripe and one thin stripe with each stroke of the roller.*

3 *Measure and mark the wall for the vertical stripes, using the width of the roller as the basis. Mark a dot for the right-hand edge of the first stripe. Allow for one set of stripes and a space of two roller widths and mark a dot for the right-hand edge of the next stripe. Mark each stripe at the top, middle, and bottom of the wall.*

4 *Using the cut roller, apply the vertical stripes. Position roller carefully at the top of the wall with the right-hand edge against the mark each time and bring it down the wall, keeping as straight as you can. Press harder as you reach the bottom of the stripe to extract paint from the roller.*

5 *With the ruler make dots to mark the top edge of each horizontal stripe. This time, leave a space of three roller widths between each set of stripes. Make several sets of marks across the wall to help you keep the roller straight.*

6 *Take the roller across the wall, positioning the top of the roller on the dot each time. Keep as straight as you can, but don't worry about any slight irregularities.*

CAFE CURTAIN

Makes a simple screen • Easy to remove and wash • Lets light into the room

A CAFE CURTAIN is a fresh and cheerful way to screen a dismal view or provide some privacy, while still allowing plenty of light into a room. Usually unlined and easy to remove and wash, café curtains are particularly suitable for kitchen windows, but can be used in any room in the house.

The simplicity of this style suits curtains with minimal fullness. Whether they are gathered, box pleated as here, or even completely flat, you should allow a little ease in the width so the curtain is not too taut on the rod.

The rod can be mounted at any height, but usually looks best in line with the center of the window frame. To attach the curtain to the rod, make a simple slot heading or eyelets through which the rod can be threaded or add sew-on rings to the top of the curtain. Perhaps the simplest method of all is to use café clips, available in many styles.

Semi-sheer
A café curtain made in a delicate fabric such as fine linen looks attractive and admits plenty of light. Instead of using clips, try attaching ribbons or ties to the pleats. They are simply looped around the rod and tied in place.

PROJECT PLANNER

2½ HOURS

Tools and Materials

Fabric: length of area of window to be covered plus 3in (7.5cm) hem allowance x width of window, plus extra width for pleats (see p.154), plus 10in (25cm) for fullness and for side hem and seam allowances • Rod to fit window • Café clips, allowing one for every pleat and one for each end • Sewing machine and thread to match fabric

1 *If necessary, join widths with a french seam (see p.134). Fold, press, and pin a 1in (2.5cm) double hem down both sides of the curtain and along the bottom edge, making mitered corners (see p.137) as shown. Machine stitch the hems.*

2 *Fold, press, and pin a ½in (12mm) double hem at the top of the curtain. The corners of the top hem do not need to be mitered. Machine stitch.*

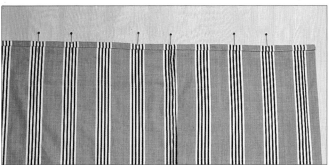

3 *Mark the positions of the pleats with pins. The width of each pleat shown here is 3in (7.5cm) and the pleats are 6in (12.5cm) apart. (See p.154 for more information on measuring and marking pleats.)*

4 *To make a pleat, fold right sides of the fabric together, so the pins marking each side of the pleat meet as shown. Place another pin 3in (7.5cm) down from the top of the curtain to hold the pleat in place and to mark the depth of stitching. Fold all the pleats in the same way.*

5 *Machine stitch each pleat along the line of the marker pins, working from the top of the curtain down to the pin marking the base of the pleat.*

6 *Press the pleats flat as shown. Attach a clip to each pleat and one to each top corner of the curtain. Thread the clip rings onto the rod.*

STENCILED TILES

New look for old tiles • Inexpensive and easy to do • Create your own design

CERAMIC TILES are expensive to replace simply because you no longer like their color, and this project is an ideal way of disguising them. First, the tiles are given a coat of primer, which prepares the surface for painting. Then the tiles are painted with vinyl latex in your chosen color. Now you can let your imagination run wild with stencils. Here, the radish and carrot echo a kitchen theme, but there are a wealth of attractive designs to choose from. Alternatively, try making stencils to your own design (see p.172 and p.184).

For the best results, be sure to place the stencils very carefully, so they are in the same position on the tile each time. Work out a pattern of blank and stenciled tiles rather than stencil every one, and keep to a limited palette of colors so the effect is not too "busy." Varnish the finished wall to protect it from moisture and wear and tear.

Kitchen partners *A carrot and radish make ideal stencil partners for this kitchen tiling. The original tiles have been covered in white latex to make a perfect backdrop for the stencil colors.*

PROJECT PLANNER

4 HOURS

Tools and Materials

Tile primer • White vinyl flat latex • Stencil paint or artist's acrylic paint in red, orange, raw umber, burnt umber, dark and light green, and white • Gloss polyurethane varnish • Ready-cut stencils or stencils made to your own design (see p.172 and p.184) • Stencil brushes • Mini-roller • Low-tack masking tape • Brush for varnish

1 *Following the manufacturer's directions, apply a coat of tile primer to tiles. Always use primer in a well-ventilated room. When the primer is dry, apply a coat of white vinyl latex to the tiles.*

2 *Take your stencils and decide on your design. Here two stencils are used, and every other tile is stenciled. If possible, cut the stencil to fit the tile. Otherwise, mark the midpoint of each tile and make sure the same part of the stencil is at the midpoint each time. Attach the stencils to the tiles with masking tape.*

3 *Using the stencil brush, stipple on the paint. For the carrot stencil used here, stipple light green onto the leaves. Add some dark green, but leave the tips light. Stipple the carrot with orange, and highlight the top edge with a little white and the bottom edge with a tiny touch of raw umber.*

4 *Stipple the leaves of the radish in light green, and add a little dark green to the undersides. Stipple the radish in red and add a little burnt umber to the bottom edge. Highlight the radish root with a touch of white. Remove the stencils and repeat the motifs as necessary.*

5 *When all the stencils are complete, leave them to dry thoroughly before varnishing. Use a roller to avoid brush marks and apply one coat of gloss polyurethane varnish.*

GARDEN ROOMS

VERDIGRIS CHAIR

Revives old furniture • Provides weatherproofing • Adds character

AN OLD METAL garden chair can be given a new lease of life with this faux verdigris technique and even coordinated with other thrift store finds. First, the chair must be carefully sanded to remove any old paint, and given a coat of rustproofing paint. The pinkness of this is then disguised with a watery coat of raw umber. The verdigris effect is simulated by dabbing the chair first with pale turquoise latex and then with dark green. The dark green should be applied in irregular patches, allowing some turquoise to show through.

Patina of time *Real verdigris is the bluish-green sheen that forms on metal as it is corroded by the elements over time. Painted verdigris mimics this look while weatherproofing the chair.*

PROJECT PLANNER

3 HOURS

Tools and Materials

Rustproofing paint • Raw umber artist's acrylic • Pale turquoise vinyl flat latex • Green vinyl flat latex • Flat polyurethane varnish • Paintbrushes • Brush for varnishing • Sandpaper • Pieces of sponge or old foam roller

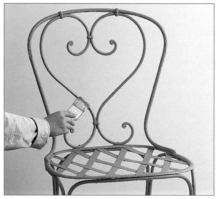

1 *Sand the chair well to remove any flakes or other debris. Apply a coat of rustproofing paint to all surfaces and let it dry for about 30 minutes.*

2 *Mix some raw umber artist's acrylic with water to a watery consistency. Paint the chair with this mixture, not to cover it, but to disguise the pinkness of the rustproofing paint.*

3 *Take some pieces of sponge or tear an old foam roller into several pieces. Using a piece of sponge or foam, dab pale turquoise vinyl latex all over the chair. Don't worry if some small areas of umber still show. Let it dry.*

4 *Take a new piece of sponge and dab dark green vinyl latex onto the chair in irregular patches so some of the paler color still shows through. Use a small brush if necessary to reach any awkward areas. Leave to dry.*

5 *Using a soft brush, apply one coat of flat-finish polyurethane varnish to the chair.*

STENCILED FLOOR RUG

Unusual floor treatment • Practical yet effective • Adaptable to space available

A PAINTED AND stenciled floor rug is a surprisingly practical way of adding color and decoration to a garden room. Once the rug is protected with varnish, it is easy to clean and wears well. It also has the advantage of being cheap to do and relatively simple to change should you tire of the design. And unlike a fabric rug, there is nothing to trip over as you walk through the room laden with plant pots.

Before you start, give careful thought to the shape of the room and the size of the floor rug. Measure the floor

carefully and plan the design to scale. It can be a simple colored shape with stencil frieze as here, or something much more complex, perhaps taking inspiration from oriental rugs.

Once the design is planned, mark the area on the floor and mask off the edges. Paint in the background color and then add the stencil frieze, positioning them with great care to keep the design neat and symmetrical. When the rug is complete, it is essential to add two coats of good-quality floor varnish to protect it from dirt and constant footsteps.

Fringe variation
The edges of the rug can be left plain (see left) or a decorative fringe can be added (see above). Using a small brush, simply add a number of fine strokes at each end of the rug. Keep the strokes close together and vary the lengths to make them look more like real fringe.

PROJECT PLANNER

2½ HOURS

Tools and Materials

Green vinyl flat latex • Artist's acrylic in three colors
• Stencils (geometric designs are most suitable)
• Stencil brushes • Paintbrush • Masking tape • Pencil
• Ruler • Polyurethane floor varnish

1 *Decide on the size you want your rug and mark it on the floor, using a pencil and ruler. The example here measures 30 x 45in (76 x 114cm).*

2 *Place masking tape all around the outside edges of the marked area. Paint the area with green vinyl latex and leave to dry. Remove the masking tape.*

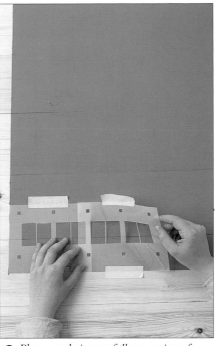

3 *Plan your design carefully on a piece of paper. Place the first stencils on the painted area. Make sure you overlap them correctly.*

4 *Using a stenciling brush, stipple in artist's acrylic paint on the stencils, using the colors in a regular design. Remove the stencils and reposition. Continue to make a frieze down both sides of the rug and at each end.*

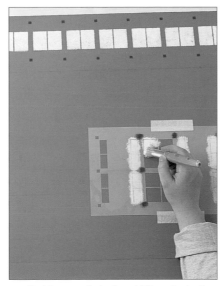

5 *Position stencils in the middle and stipple in colors. Repeat as required, again making sure you overlap the stencils correctly.*

6 *Allow the stenciling to dry. Apply two coats of good-quality polyurethane floor varnish over the whole rug to protect it.*

BOLSTER

Simple to make • Adds comfort to hard seating • Distinctive tie feature

A BOLSTER IS A long cylindrical cushion. In the past, bolsters covered in opulent fabric were used to luxurious effect on chaise longues and daybeds in chic drawing rooms. Brought up to date, however, they are not at all out of place in the one room in a modern home designed specifically for relaxation and leisure – the garden room. Cover the bolsters in a more robust fabric than the silks and brocades of old, and place them at each end of sturdy bench seating or on wooden garden furniture. An extra-long bolster could also make a comfortable back rest on a hard garden bench.

This bolster cover is made as a simple long tube to fit the circumference of the bolster pad, and a zipper is inserted into the long seam. Each end of the cover is then turned in and gathered to form a self-lined frill of fabric. To give this bolster cushion a special garden twist, use a lively green striped fabric and tie each end of the cover with ordinary green garden twine.

Tassel ties
Easy to make, tassels in garden twine hold the bolster cover's gathers in place and add a distinctive touch. Alternatively, use silk, wool, or cotton, or simply tie the ends of the bolster with two lengths of tasseled rope.

PROJECT PLANNER

2¾ HOURS

Tools and Materials

Standard bolster pad 18in (46cm) long with a diameter of 7in (18cm) • Fabric: length of bolster plus diameter, plus 14in (36cm) for ruffle x circumference of bolster plus 1¼in (3cm) seam allowance (see p.130 for information on measuring bolster) • 14in (36cm) zipper • Garden twine for ties • Sewing machine and thread to match fabric

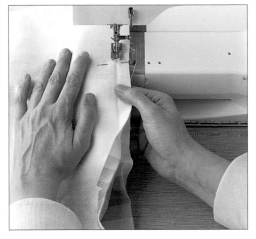

1 *Fold the fabric in half lengthwise, right sides together. Mark the position of the zipper in the center of the long side. Machine stitch to the beginning of the zipper, making a ⅝in (1.5cm) seam allowance, and backstitch to secure. Machine stitch below the zipper; backstitch to secure. Insert the zipper (see p.153).*

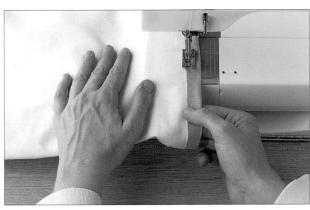

2 *At the end of the cover, press a ⅝in (1.5cm) hem and machine stitch. Repeat at the other end.*

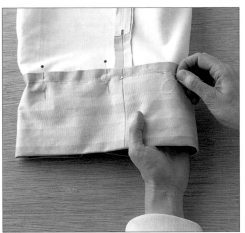

3 *Turn another 3½in (9cm) to the wrong side and press. Using large running stitches (see p.138), sew around just below the line of machine stitching. Push the needle through to the right side and leave the loose thread. Repeat at the other end and turn the cushion right side out.*

4 *Pull up the gathering as tightly as you can. Re-thread the needle and secure the stitching. Repeat at the other end of the bolster cover.*

5 *Push the cushion pad into the cover through the zipper opening – it should be a tight fit. Make two tassels from a ball of garden twine (see p.157). Cut a piece of garden twine 3ft (1m) long and attach a tassel to each end. Wind the twine around and around the end of the cover, gathering it as tightly as possible, and tie. Fluff out the ruffle. Repeat at the other end of the bolster.*

DISTRESSED DOOR

Adds a naturally aged look • Disguises a scruffy door • Quick and easy

THIS TECHNIQUE recreates the look of paintwork that has darkened and become worn and cracked over time. It can be used to age a new door or disguise battered old wood and gives a pleasantly countrified and informal feel, particularly well suited to a garden room. The door is painted with a coat of dark green latex and furniture wax is then applied to areas that would receive the hardest wear and tear. A coat of cream paint is applied over the green, and the waxed areas are rubbed with steel wool to give a naturally worn look.

A country look *Distressed paintwork makes this old farmhouse door an ideal partner for the rustic brick walls and casual atmosphere of this pleasant garden room.*

PROJECT PLANNER

2½ HOURS

Tools and Materials
Dark green vinyl flat latex • Cream vinyl flat latex • Steel wool • Furniture wax • Paintbrushes • Rubber gloves • Sandpaper • Cheesecloth

1 Sand the door carefully to remove any rough areas and create a smooth surface.

2 Apply a coat of dark green vinyl latex to the door. The coverage can be quite rough. Let it dry for 30 minutes.

3 Take a rag or cheesecloth and apply furniture wax to the areas you want to look distressed. Concentrate on those that are likely to be particularly worn, such as the area around the latch and the central stile.

4 Apply a coat of cream vinyl latex to the door and leave it to dry for 30 minutes. Again, the finish does not have to be perfect.

5 Always wear rubber gloves when working with steel wool. Take a big pad of steel wool and rub the areas where you applied wax – these will appear slightly whiter than the rest of the door. Rub them vigorously until the green shows through. Keep rubbing until the door has a naturally aged look.

TOPIARY MURAL

A simple way to make a mural • Fun to look at • Highly individual

THE CLEAN, GRAPHIC shapes of this topiary mural are a perfect decoration for the wall of a conservatory or garden room. And you do not even need any artistic ability – the basic shapes are simply photocopies that are pasted onto the wall.

Start by photocopying and enlarging the templates at the back of this book. Alternatively, draw some of your own, but remember that simple designs will look best. The shapes are painted with watery washes of terra-cotta and green and

carefully cut out. They are then pasted onto the wall, with care taken to space them evenly and overlap the sections in the same way each time. The mural can extend around the whole room, or you may prefer to have only three or four trees positioned in the center of one wall.

Green simplicity *Simple and stylish, this row of topiary shapes makes an entertaining and highly individual addition to the real greenery in a garden room.*

88

PROJECT PLANNER

4 HOURS

Tools and Materials
Photocopies of the templates on p.182 or of your chosen designs • Burnt umber artist's acrylic paint • Green artist's acrylic paint • Craft glue • Flat-finish varnish • Large artist's brush • Paintbrush • Scissors • Ruler • Pencil

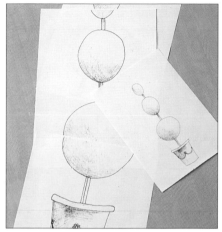

1 *Photocopy the topiary templates on p.182 or the designs of your choice to the required size. You may need to photocopy the image in several sections to make it big enough. Figure out where the shapes are to be placed on the wall and mark in pencil the base line and spacing between each one.*

2 *Mix burnt umber artist's acrylic with water to make a thin terra-cotta wash. Using a big artist's brush, wash the terra-cotta over the pots and the plant stems. It doesn't matter if you go over the edges because you are going to cut the images out. Mix a watery green wash and apply to the plant sections. Leave the shapes to dry.*

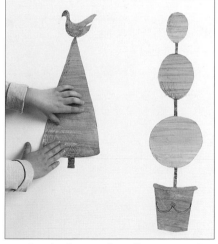

3 *Using sharp scissors, cut out the shapes very carefully. If they look very wrinkled, try ironing them on the back.*

4 *Using glue, paste the back of a shape. Don't apply the glue too thickly, but make sure the whole area is covered.*

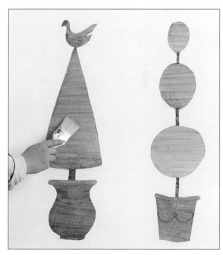

5 *Place the shape on the wall. Starting in the center and working out, smooth it down as much as possible. Wrinkles generally disappear as the glue dries. Overlap the separate parts slightly so there is no gap. Continue placing the designs, making sure each one is sitting on the same base line and that there is equal space between them.*

6 *Leave until the glue is completely dry and then apply a coat of flat varnish over each topiary shape to finish.*

DIRECTOR'S CHAIR

Practical and pretty • Personalizes your chairs • Revives old covers

PERSONALIZE AN ordinary director's chair with the fabric of your choice. All director's chairs have two canvas slings that are held on the wooden frame to form the seat and back of the chair. The method by which they are attached varies slightly, but on most chairs the slings are slotted onto the frame for ease of removal. The slings have to be made of canvas, or some other sturdy fabric, in order to support the weight of an adult. This limits your choice, so cover the existing canvas with another fabric. Remove the canvas slings before starting the project.

Weather protection *To give the covered chair some protection from the elements when it is used outdoors, spray each covered sling with fabric protector back and front before reassembling.*

PROJECT PLANNER

1¼ HOURS

Tools and Materials
Fabric for two back pieces: 1x the depth of canvas back plus 1¼in (3cm) x width of back plus 6¼in (16cm) and 1 x the depth of canvas back plus 1½in (3cm) by the width of the back less the slots plus 1¼in (3cm) • Fabric for seat: depth of canvas seat plus 2in (5cm) x width of seat (excluding slots) plus ¾in (2cm) • Sewing machine and thread to match fabric

Seat

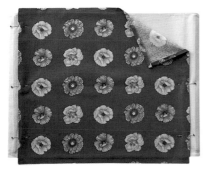  

1 *Press ⅜in (1cm) to the wrong side on all sides of the fabric. Place the canvas seat right side up and center the fabric on top of it, right side up. The folded edges at the sides of the fabric should come just to the beginning of the canvas slots. Pin the fabric to the canvas at the sides.*

2 *Machine stitch down each side, keeping close to the folded edge. Take the wood out of the canvas slot first or if you can't, use a zipper foot on the machine.*

3 *Fold the pressed hem allowance at the top and bottom of the fabric over to the wrong side of the canvas and pin. Machine stitch in place.*

Back

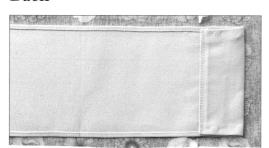  

1 *Place the larger piece of fabric right side down and center the canvas, also right side down, on top. Clip the seam allowance of the fabric to align with the inside edge of the canvas slots.*

2 *At the top and bottom, fold the ⅝in (1.5cm) seam allowance over to the wrong side of the canvas and pin. Secure temporarily with basting (see p.138). Starting at the cut in the seam allowance, fold over the seam allowance at the top and bottom of the rest of the fabric (see inset).*

3 *Fold the fabric around the slots, angling it in slightly as shown, and pin. Hand sew the fabric to the canvas all around the top and bottom of the slot using uneven slipstitch (see p.138). Repeat at the other end of the back section.*

4 *Take the smaller piece of fabric and press under a ⅝in (1.5cm) seam allowance all around. With the right side facing up, pin it onto the back of the back section to cover the canvas. Make sure each end comes just where the slot begins and covers the raw edges of the first piece of fabric.*

5 *Machine stitch through all layers, keeping close to the folded edges of the smaller back section. Remove the basting.*

BEDROOMS

APPLIQUED BED LINEN

Makes plain linen special • Color coordinates your bedroom • Inexpensive to make

DESPITE THE WIDE choice of bed linen designs on the market, it can still be hard to find something to coordinate with today's subtle color palette in designs that won't overpower a peaceful bedroom.

One solution is to buy an ordinary set of plain white cotton bed linen and embellish it with a delicate appliquéd design in the colors of your choice. Appliqué is not difficult if you use iron-on adhesive webbing, sold in most craft and fabric stores. The webbing comes on a paper backing onto which you can draw or trace your design. Iron it onto the wrong side of your appliqué fabric, peel off the backing, and then iron the shape directly onto the bed linen. Follow the manufacturer's directions for precise iron temperature settings and timings. Once the appliqué is ironed on, it will stay in place while you outline the design in machine satin stitch, making your task much easier.

Ribbon appliqué
Another way to make plain white bed linen something special is to attach pretty colored ribbons (above). Machine stitch the ribbon along the top and bottom edges.

PROJECT PLANNER

Tools and Materials
Plain bed linen: sheet, two pillowcases • Fabric for appliqué: ¼ yd (¼m) of each color • Fusible webbing • Paper for template (see p.180) • Sewing machine and thread to match or contrast with fabric

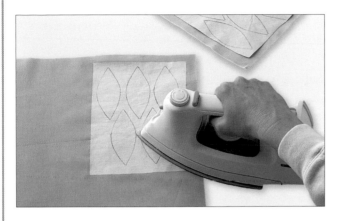

1 *Copy the leaf template on p.180 and draw shapes onto the fusible webbing. Iron the webbing onto wrong side of appliqué fabric, following the manufacturer's directions. Prepare some in blue and some in green fabric.*

2 *Cut out all of the leaves carefully. Peel the paper backing off each one and set aside, adhesive side up.*

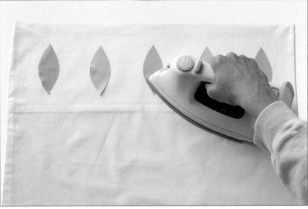

3 *Take one pillowcase. Position the leaves along the open end of the pillowcase, starting with the center leaf. Work outward, making sure all of the leaves are evenly spaced. When you are happy with the arrangement, iron the leaves in place, following the webbing manufacturer's directions.*

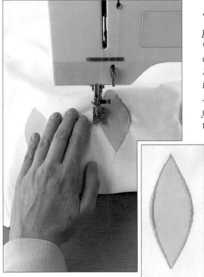

4 *Next, the leaves must be satin stitched (see p.135) – practice on a scrap of fabric first. Open out the pillowcase so you don't stitch through both layers. Set the stitch width to zero and the stitch length to just above zero. Start stitching and gradually increase the stitch width to medium in the middle of the leaf. Taper it down so it is back to zero when you reach the point. At the point, pivot the work and stitch down the other side of the leaf the same way (see inset). Continue until you have satin-stitched all of the leaves.*

5 *Draw a wavy line lightly in pencil below the leaves and satin stitch (see p.135). Start at zero, work up to medium, and then taper back to zero at the end (see inset). Repeat Steps 2 to 5 at the top of your sheet.*

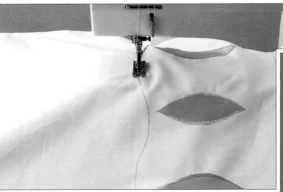

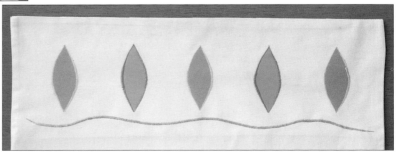

95

Two-tone Stenciled Wall

Adds interest to a plain wall • Divides a wall • Easy to adapt to your own design

PAINTING A WALL in two different tones adds character and helps ground a room. The stronger shade should always be below the dado and the tones should be closely related, like these two lilacs – bold, contrasting colors would be disruptive.

Additional interest is provided here by the delicately stenciled insect frieze above the dado. The frieze uses just three colors in a repeating pattern to create a consistent and harmonious design. The frieze has been kept small so that it does not overwhelm the room.

Optional extras *Here and there, an extra insect breaking out of the frieze prevents the pattern from becoming monotonous. Don't overdo it, however – less is more in this instance.*

PROJECT PLANNER

3½ HOURS

Tools and Materials
White undercoat • Deep lilac and pale lilac vinyl flat latex (or colors of your choice) • Blue, yellow, white, and green artist's acrylic paint • Insect stencil frieze • Low-tack masking tape • Three small stencil brushes • Paintbrushes

1 *Prepare the wall (see p. 169) and apply white undercoat unless the wall is white already. Leave it to dry. Place a strip of masking tape along the top of the dado rail, butting up to where the wall and dado meet. Paint the upper part of the wall in the paler shade of vinyl latex and leave it to dry. Remove the masking tape.*

2 *Place a strip of masking tape just above the dado rail. Paint the lower half of the wall and the dado in the darker shade of vinyl latex. Remove the masking tape and leave it to dry.*

3 *Working from the right, anchor the stencil to the wall with masking tape. Make sure the lower edge of the stencil is straight and position it on the dado each time. Using a small stencil brush, stipple paint onto the stencil. Hold the brush at a right angle to the wall and apply paint with dabbing motions.*

4 *Vary the color combinations, giving, for example, one butterfly blue wings and a yellow body and another green wings and a blue body. Keep to the limited palette of three colors and white to give your design consistency.*

5 *When the first section of the frieze is complete, remove and reposition the stencil. Tape it in place exactly where the first section finished so the spacing is correct, and continue stippling on paint with dabbing motions as before. To keep the design consistent, repeat the same color combinations in each section of the frieze.*

LINED BASKETS

Quick to make • Inexpensive storage method • Versatile and attractive

FOR A PRACTICAL and pretty storage solution for clothes and linen in the bedroom, use wicker baskets of varying sizes and stack them on deep shelves. Make simple fabric linings to tie inside the baskets to protect your delicate items of clothing from catching and snagging on the wickerwork.

Almost any fabric can be used. Coordinate the basket linings with any of the other textiles in the bedroom, for instance, or use a feminine floral chintz with narrow satin ribbons for ties. For a country look, choose bright gingham or ticking stripes, or go for quiet simplicity with starched white linen and natural linen tape like the ones shown here. Make sure the fabric you choose is washable. If there is any risk of shrinkage, wash the fabric before you start to make the linings.

The basket linings are simple to make. The fabric is cut out, following the diagram opposite and the dimensions of the basket, and stitched together at the corners. The ties are then attached at each corner, and the top of the lining is turned over and machine stitched.

Decorative linings
Slender ties are threaded through gaps in the wickerwork and fastened in a bow to hold the lining in place.

PROJECT PLANNER

1¼ HOURS

Tools and Materials

Fabric for one: the length of basket plus twice the depth plus 1½in (4cm) seam allowances x the width of basket plus twice the depth plus 1½in (4cm) seam allowances • 2½yd (2.5m) linen tape or ribbon for ties • Sewing machine and thread to match fabric

Plan for liner fabric

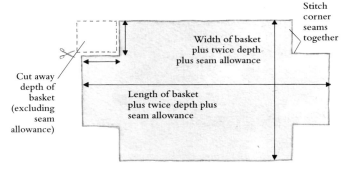

Stitch corner seams together

Width of basket plus twice depth plus seam allowance

Cut away depth of basket (excluding seam allowance)

Length of basket plus twice depth plus seam allowance

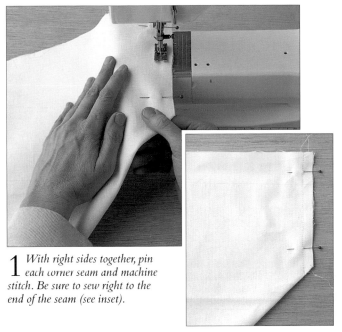

1 *With right sides together, pin each corner seam and machine stitch. Be sure to sew right to the end of the seam (see inset).*

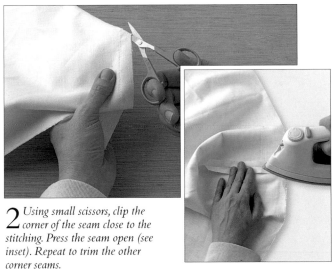

2 *Using small scissors, clip the corner of the seam close to the stitching. Press the seam open (see inset). Repeat to trim the other corner seams.*

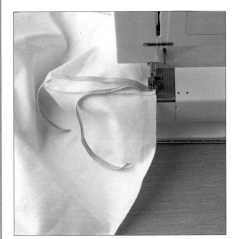

3 *Cut four ties each about 24in (60cm) long. Fold one tie in half and pin with the folded edge at the top of a corner seam. Machine stitch across the top of the tie, keeping very close to the top of the fabric. Repeat to attach the other ties.*

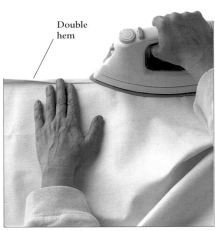

Double hem

4 *Fold over a ⅜in (1cm) double hem at the top edge of the basket lining. Press and pin.*

5 *Machine stitch all around the hem, keeping close to the folded edge and keeping the ends of the ties out of the way.*

BED CANOPY

A dramatic feature • Simple to make • Adds luxury and comfort

A BED CANOPY IS a delightful way to enjoy large swags of beautiful fabric. This canopy is hung from two bamboo poles cut a little wider than the bed. One is mounted close to the wall above the bed, and the other is suspended by cord or chain from two hooks attached to the ceiling. The second pole can be placed to form a half-tester canopy as here or can carry the fabric the full length of the bed. To check the amount of fabric you need, put up the poles and run a length of string from the floor up and over the poles (see diagram opposite).

Choosing fabric *Practically any fabric could be used, from heavy woven kilim to the flimsiest voile, but make sure the poles you use can support the weight of the fabric.*

PROJECT PLANNER

4 HOURS

Tools and Materials

Main fabric (join widths if necessary): to fit width of bed plus 1¼in (3cm) seam allowance x 4¼yd (3.85m) • Lining: as main fabric • Two poles to fit width of bed plus 8in (20cm) • Two skeins of silk embroidery floss • Touch-and-close tape • Sewing machine and thread to match fabric

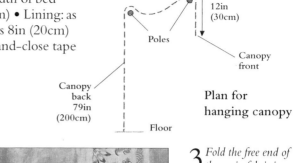

36in (90cm)

12in (30cm)

Poles

Canopy front

Canopy back 79in (200cm)

Floor

Plan for hanging canopy

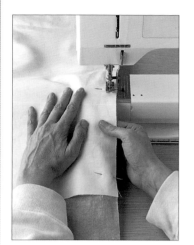

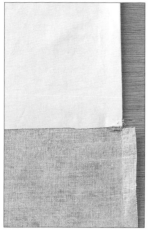

1 *With right sides together, pin main fabric and lining along the side seams, leaving 24in (60cm) at one end of the main fabric unlined. Machine stitch, making ⅝in (1.5cm) seam allowances.*

2 *Turn right side out and clip the seam allowance of the main fabric just below the lining. Repeat on the other side.*

3 *Fold the free end of the main fabric in half, right sides together, taking the fabric to just above the notch and pin in place. Machine stitch at each side from the base of the lining to the fold of the fabric (see inset). Turn right side out and press.*

4 *Turn the canopy over and, using a wide zigzag, machine stitch over the seam between the lining and the main fabric to finish the raw edge neatly.*

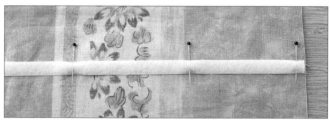

5 *Turn the work back to the right side and pin a strip of touch-and-close tape (soft side) over the line of zigzag stitching. Machine stitch along the top and bottom of the strip.*

6 *Measure the distance between the two poles and mark the position of the second touch-and-close strip. Pin the strip in position on the main fabric and machine stitch top and bottom. Staple hard (hook) side of strip to the tops of the poles.*

7 *Make silk tassels (see p.156) and stitch one to each front corner of the canopy.*

STIPPLED WALLS

Subtle textured effect • Conceals irregularities • Creates a warm, friendly look

ONE OF THE SIMPLEST of all paint effects to achieve, stippling gives a wall texture and interest. It is also useful for concealing any irregularities in the plasterwork and brings a warm, friendly look to a room. The wall is painted white and then glazed in sections, using a mixture of latex, scumble glaze, and water. A stippling brush is used to work over the wet paint, leaving lots of tiny brushmarks and lifting some of the glaze to create a subtle effect. You do need to work quickly to stipple the paint while it is wet – a helper can make the task much easier.

Cozy pink *As a flat color, this glowing bright pink might overwhelm, but the stippling technique and white ground makes it a perfect choice for a warm, cozy bedroom.*

PROJECT PLANNER

1½ HOURS

Tools and Materials
White vinyl flat latex • Vinyl flat latex in chosen color • Scumble glaze • Paintbrushes • Stipple brush

1 *Prepare the wall (see p. 169) and apply a coat of white vinyl latex to the whole area (see p. 166). Leave it to dry for 30 minutes.*

2 *Mix a glaze with the chosen color, using vinyl latex, scumble glaze, and water (see p. 165). Using a brush, apply the mixture to the first section of the wall (see p. 170) with rough crisscrossing strokes.*

3 *While the paint is still wet, use a stippling brush to work over the painted section with quick pouncing movements. The tips of the bristles leave lots of tiny imprints in the wet glaze. Try to avoid working in lines. If you do make a line of stippling, go over it in another direction.*

4 *Work quickly and apply glaze to the next section while the edge of the first is still wet (see p. 170). If you let the edges dry, you will get telltale join-up marks. Continue glazing and stippling as in Steps 2 and 3 until the wall is complete.*

HEADBOARD COVER

Disguises an ugly headboard • Provides cushioning comfort • Adds visual appeal

FUN TO LOOK AT and simple to make, this slip-on headboard cover makes a hard metal or wooden headboard soft and comfortable. If you don't have a headboard, you could cut a similar shape out of blockboard and screw it to the end of the bed base.

It is important to make sure the cover fits well. To do this, fold your fabric in half and lay the headboard down on top of it. Using chalk, trace around the shape directly onto the fabric, then cut out both panels, leaving a 2in (5cm) seam allowance. Put the headboard back behind the bed and pin the front and back panels of the cover together on the headboard. Make sure the cover fits closely, but that you can still slide it on and off. Bear in mind that there will be a layer of thick batting inside the cover to pad it out. When you are happy with the fit, trim the remaining seam allowance to within ¾in (2cm) of your pinned seamline.

Gingham heart headboard *This cover is made of durable stonewashed denim, piped and appliquéd with gingham, but any sturdy washable fabric could be used.*

PROJECT PLANNER

3 HOURS

Tools and Materials

Main fabric: two panels to fit headboard plus ¾in (2cm) seam and hem allowances all around • Appliqué and piping fabric: see heart template on p.180 and piping instructions on p.147 and p.150 • 9oz (255g) batting to fit headboard • Iron-on fusible webbing • Spray adhesive • Piping cord • Sewing machine and thread to match fabric

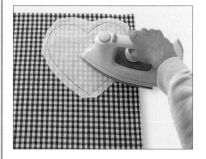

1 Draw the heart shape (see template on p.180) on paper side of the fusible webbing. Cut out roughly and place on the wrong side of the appliqué fabric, adhesive side down. If using patterned fabric, make sure the shape is centered on the pattern. Iron the webbing onto the fabric.

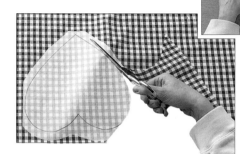

2 Cut out the shape carefully, keeping close to pencil line. Peel off the paper backing (see inset) and set the heart aside, adhesive side up.

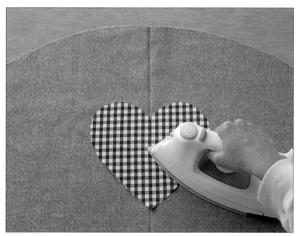

3 Take one panel of the main fabric, fold it in half, and press to mark the midpoint. Place the panel right side up and position the appliqué on the panel, adhesive side down. Make sure the center of the heart is on the central crease of the main fabric and about 4in (10cm) down from the top. Smooth the appliqué down and iron it in position.

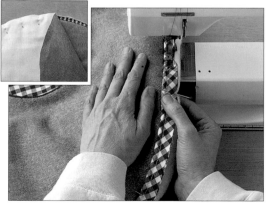

4 The fusible adhesive holds the appliqué shape in position while you stitch. Using satin stitch (see p.135), machine stitch all around the edge of the heart.

5 Cut the batting the same size as the headboard fabric, less base hem allowance. Place the top fabric panel wrong side up and roll the batting over it to check for size; trim if necessary. Roll batting back, spray wrong side of the fabric with adhesive, and roll the batting back down over fabric.

6 Make piping (see p.150) to fit the curved edge of the headboard. Using a zipper foot, machine stitch the piping to the right side of the front panel, keeping close to the line of stitching on the piping (see p.150). Then place the back panel of the cover onto the front panel, right sides together, and pin (see inset), leaving base hem open. Machine stitch front and back panels together.

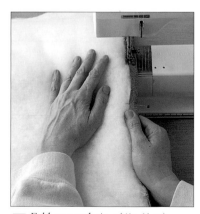

7 Fold over and pin a ½in (1cm) double hem all around the base of the cover, making sure you catch the edge of the batting. Machine stitch the hem in place. Using slipstitch (see p.138), hand sew the ends of the piping to the back of the hem. Turn the cover right side out.

SIMPLE QUILT

Light but cozy • Made by hand • An attractive extra layer

THIS COZY QUILT makes a useful extra layer or a lightweight cover for the summer months. It is made from one piece of fabric bonded to polyester batting, with another contrasting piece of fabric laid underneath and folded up and over the raw edges. The layers are quilted together with small disks of wool or felt, stitched in place with french knots. To estimate the size, measure the made-up bed and allow for a generous cover.

Use fabric that feels soft to the touch, particularly for the underneath layer. As always, when you are using several different fabrics together, check that they are preshrunk and colorfast. Wash them all beforehand to make sure.

Textural interest *The quilt here is made from fabrics with contrasting textures rather than pattern to create interest – a strong cotton waffle teamed with a smooth checked lightweight cotton.*

PROJECT PLANNER

Tools and Materials

Fabric for top panel: to fit bed • Fabric for bottom panel: finished size
of quilt plus 1½in (4cm) all around • 4oz (113g) batting cut to finished size of quilt
plus 1in (2.5cm) all around • Embellishments: 10in (25cm) of contrasting fabric
• Embroidery floss • Basting spray • Thread to match fabric

3 HOURS

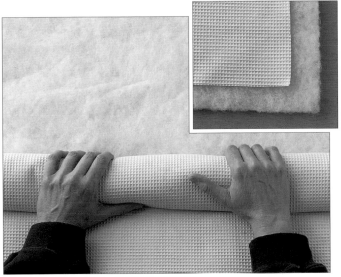

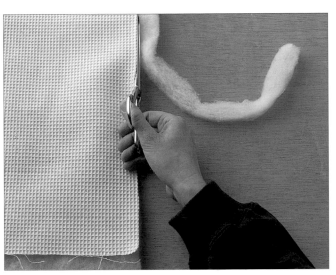

1 *Roll up the main panel fabric. Lay the batting down and place the fabric over it, wrong side down to check size. The batting will extend beyond the edge of the fabric (see inset), but will be trimmed to fit. Roll the fabric back again and spray the batting with basting spray. Working quickly but carefully, unroll the batting over the fabric.*

2 *Trim off the excess batting to fit the fabric exactly. Note that it is better to have too much batting and trim it to fit than to try to calculate the exact amount.*

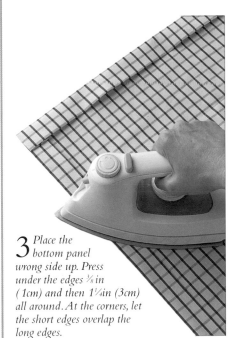

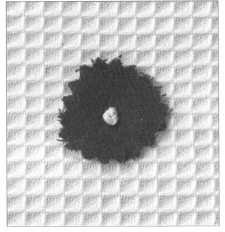

3 *Place the bottom panel wrong side up. Press under the edges ⅜in (1cm) and then 1¼in (3cm) all around. At the corners, let the short edges overlap the long edges.*

4 *With the batting face down, place the top panel over the bottom panel, tucking the edges under the folded edges of the bottom panel. Neatly slipstitch (see p.138) the folded edges of the bottom panel to the top fabric.*

5 *Measure your quilt and decide how many embellishments you want to add. Measure and mark their positions. Make the embellishments (see p.157) and stitch each one in place through all layers of fabric with a french knot (see p.139) in embroidery floss.*

CLOUD DOOR

Easy and fun • Perfect for a child's room • Adds a decorative feature

THIS IS A WONDERFUL finish for a door in a child's bedroom and should help to induce sweet dreams. It creates a magical effect that you don't need to be an expert artist to achieve – anyone can paint clouds.

When you apply the blue glaze to the door, try to keep the color stronger at the top, gradually decreasing toward the bottom. Don't apply the clouds too heavily – they should be delicate and slightly translucent like the real things. Vary the shapes of the clouds, and make sure that you have some coming in from each side of the door.

Blue skies *Puffy white clouds on a bright blue sky make an ordinary bedroom door into a cheerful feature and shouldn't tax anyone's artistic skills.*

PROJECT PLANNER

3½ HOURS

Tools and Materials
White satin latex • Blue artist's acrylic • White artist's acrylic • Scumble glaze • Gloss polyurethane varnish • Paintbrushes • Softening brush

1 *If the door is already painted, sand it thoroughly. Apply a coat of white satin latex and let it dry for at least 30 minutes.*

2 *Mix a glaze with blue artist's acrylic, scumble glaze, and water (see p. 165). Apply the glaze in sections, starting at the top of the door and using horizontal strokes to work back and forth across the door. Use plenty of paint so the section at the top of the door appears to be the darkest.*

3 *While the first section of glaze is still damp, go over it with a softening brush to disguise the brush marks. Once the first section is softened, continue painting and softening the door in sections. Use slightly less paint as you work down the door so it becomes lighter toward the bottom.*

4 *Using a small amount of white artist's acrylic paint, start making the clouds with swirling, rounded strokes. Indicate the main shape of the cloud first and then add more white, but don't let them get too heavy – they should retain some translucency.*

5 *With a little more white paint on the brush than before, add some white highlights to the edges of the clouds. Be careful not to overdo it. Leave it to dry for an hour.*

6 *Apply a coat of gloss polyurethane varnish to the finished door and leave it to dry completely.*

BATHROOMS

BATHROOM ORGANIZER

A stylish way of storing clutter • Adaptable pocket sizes • Waterproof finish

H ERE IS A HANDY hanging organizer in which to store the many odds and ends that tend to clutter a bathroom. You can make the organizer the exact size shown here or adapt it to fit your own requirements, with pockets designed to accommodate particular items. Choose two stylish but sturdy coordinating fabrics. Spray both with fabric protector to give the cloth a water-resistant finish before you start to assemble the organizer or choose vinyl-coated fabric. Hang the finished organizer behind a door or from hooks on the wall. Alternatively, if you prefer to hang the organizer on a towel rod, make long ties instead of loops at the top.

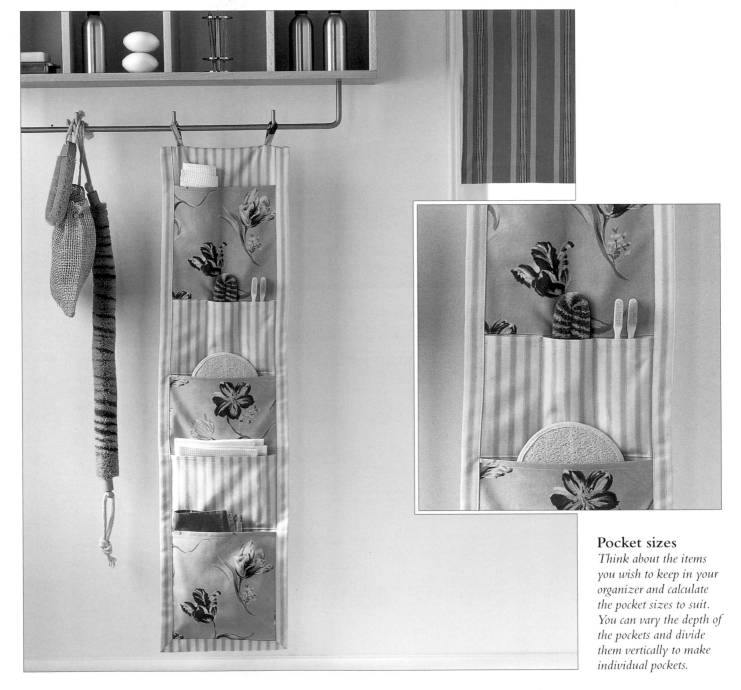

Pocket sizes

Think about the items you wish to keep in your organizer and calculate the pocket sizes to suit. You can vary the depth of the pockets and divide them vertically to make individual pockets.

PROJECT PLANNER

2 HOURS

Tools and Materials

Fabric for main panels: one top panel 12 x 46in (30 x 116.5cm) and one base panel 16 x 50in (40 x 121.5cm) • Fabric for pockets: two pockets 12 x 12in (30 x 30cm) and three pockets 8 x 12in (20 x 30cm) • Fabric for two bias-cut ties with finished size of ½ x 10in (12mm x 25cm) (see p.148) • Fabric protector spray • Sewing machine and thread to match fabric

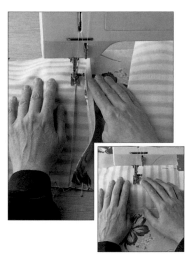

1 *Before starting to sew, spray both sides of all pieces of fabric with fabric protector to make them water resistant. Follow the manufacturer's directions when spraying.*

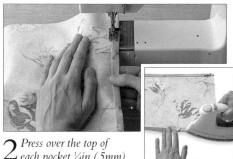

2 *Press over the top of each pocket ¼in (5mm) and then ⅜in (1cm) and pin. Machine stitch close to the folded edge. Press over the bottom edge of all except the bottom pocket ⅝in (1.5cm) (see inset).*

3 *Place the top panel right side up. Starting at the bottom, place the pockets right side up on the panel, butting them up to one another, and leaving about 4in (10cm) free at the top. Pin in place.*

4 *Machine stitch across the base of each pocket, working close to the folded edge each time. When you reach the bottom pocket, stitch it with the bottom edge flat, not folded. Divide one pocket into two and another into three by machine stitching from top to bottom (see inset). Backstitch at the start and finish to secure the stitching.*

5 *Make two bias cut ties (see p.148), each ½in (12mm) wide by 10in (25cm) long. Fold each tie in half and position at the top of the top panel, raw edges aligned. Machine stitch across the ties to hold them in place.*

6 *Take the base panel. Press over 1in (2.5cm) double hems at the sides and base, mitering corners (see p.137).*

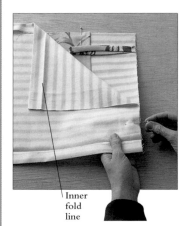

Inner fold line

7 *With right sides together, place the base panel over the top panel, aligning centers. Open out the folds on the base panel and pin the panels together across the top. Machine stitch ⅝in (1.5cm) from the top, starting from the inner fold line of the base panel and stitching across to the other inner fold line.*

8 *Fold the base panel over to the back. Tuck the top panel under the folded edges of the base panel and pin the panels together along sides and base.*

9 *Machine stitch all around. Start at the top corner and, keeping close to the inner folded edge, stitch down one side, around the corner, and across the base and then up the other side. Hand sew the diagonal corners using even slipstitch (see p.138).*

COMBED BATHTUB

Transforms plain panel • Coordinates with room decor • Easy to do

THIS SIMPLE, BUT highly effective technique is a perfect way of bringing decorative interest to a plain or unattractive bathtub. Colored latex is applied over a white base and a homemade cardboard comb is dragged though the paint while it is still wet. The comb lifts off some of the top coat of paint, revealing the white beneath. Here the comb is dragged down the panel and then across to create a crisscrossing pattern. The finished effect is slightly irregular in places, but this is part of the charm of the technique.

Color combinations *Greenish-blue and white make a perfect bathroom color scheme, but any combination of colors can be used. Make sure the base coat is lighter than the top coat.*

PROJECT PLANNER

2½ HOURS

Tools and Materials
Undercoat • White vinyl flat latex • Vinyl flat latex in chosen color • Flat polyurethane varnish • Thick cardboard for comb (see p.173) • Knife • Ruler • Pencil • Paintbrushes • Soft brush for varnishing

1 *Make a comb from thick, sturdy cardboard. (See p.173 for more information on making and cutting the comb.)*

2 *If the bathtub is not already white, apply an undercoat. Then apply one coat of white vinyl latex and let it dry.*

3 *Apply a coat of vinyl latex in your chosen color to a section of the bathtub.*

4 *While the paint is still wet, take the comb and draw it firmly down through the paint, lifting off some of the top coat to reveal the white below. Comb the whole section, placing the comb next to the previous line of combing each time. Have a rag on hand and wipe the excess paint off the comb after each line.*

5 *Then drag the comb across the section, placing it next to the previous line of combing each time. Work quickly before the paint dries. Apply vinyl latex to the next section and comb as before. Continue until the whole panel has been painted and combed and leave it to dry thoroughly.*

6 *Using a soft brush, apply a coat of flat-finish polyurethane varnish to the finished panel to protect the paintwork.*

SHOWER CURTAIN

Simple but effective • Make to fit your shower • Individual design

CREATE YOUR OWN shower curtain from stark white vinyl and chrome eyelets, but add a feminine touch with a pretty lace effect edging down each side of the curtain. If you have white tiles, think of using colored material or the lace effect will be lost. Vinyl fabric is only available in one width, but if you need to screen off the length of a bathtub, make two curtains that meet in the middle. Experiment with the template on spare fabric before you start so you are sure to get it right on the real thing. Try varying the pattern with scallops, but keep it simple.

A lacy look *The lace effect, made using pinking shears and a leather punch, is very effective, particularly when set against colored tiles or paint effects around your bath or shower.*

PROJECT PLANNER

Tools and Materials

Main fabric (vinyl or similar waterproof material): measure the distance from the curtain rod to the floor and add 2in (5cm) for top hem x width of fabric or 1¼ times curtain rod • Cardboard for template • Water-based felt pen • Pinking shears • Leather punch • Eyelet kit • Hammer

2½ HOURS

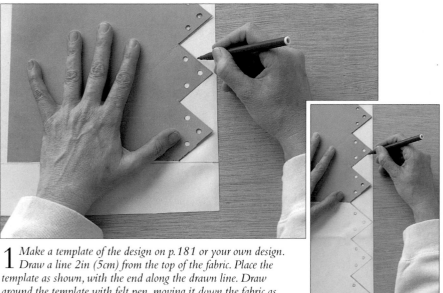

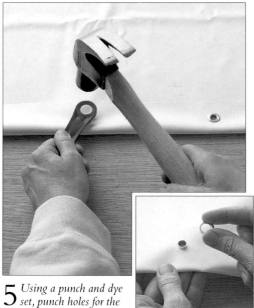

1 *Make a template of the design on p.181 or your own design. Draw a line 2in (5cm) from the top of the fabric. Place the template as shown, with the end along the drawn line. Draw around the template with felt pen, moving it down the fabric as required (see inset). Mark holes with dots.*

2 *Using a pair of pinking shears, trim off the end above the drawn line as shown. Then cut around the line of the template.*

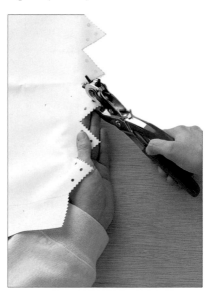

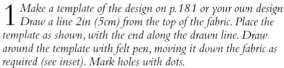

3 *Use a leather punch to carefully punch out all the marked holes. Repeat Steps 1 to 3 down the other side of the curtain.*

4 *Turn the fabric over at the marked fold line. Mark the position of the first eyelet about 1in (2.5cm) in from the end. Mark the positions of the remaining eyelets at approximately 6in (15cm) intervals across the top of the curtain.*

5 *Using a punch and dye set, punch holes for the eyelets at the marked positions, following the directions with your kit. Insert the base of the eyelet through the hole from the right side of the curtain. Place the backing ring over the top (see inset) and hammer on. Clean off any marks.*

MOSAIC SPLASH PROTECTOR

Colorful • Decorative yet practical • Easy to adapt

PRACTICAL AND pretty, mosaic tiles make perfect splash protection for a bathroom hand basin. These little tiles are available in a wide selection of colors and can be arranged to suit your taste and color scheme. It is best to construct the splash protector on a piece of sturdy composite board and put the completed item up on the wall. To make the splash protector even more waterproof,

apply a layer of watered-down white craft glue over the tile adhesive before starting to put the tiles in place. This helps seal the splash protector against moisture damage.

Eye-catching and adaptable *Neat and colorful, this arrangement of mosaic tiles makes an eye-catching splash protector that is easy to adapt to your own design.*

PROJECT PLANNER

9½ HOURS

Tools and Materials

Piece of ⅛in (3mm) composite board to fit back of sink x 14–16in (35–40cm) high • Mosaic tiles in chosen colors • Tile adhesive • Ready-mixed grouting • Squeegy tool • Utility knife • Old kitchen knife or palette knife for spreading adhesive • Sponge • Dry cloth

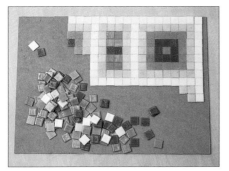

1 *Soak the tiles in water to remove the paper backing. Decide on your design by arranging the tiles on the board. Allow a ⅟₁₆in (2mm) space between each tile.*

2 *Using a utility knife, score the surface of the board with crisscrossing diagonal lines. This helps the tile adhesive stick to the surface.*

3 *Spread a thin layer of tile adhesive over the scored side of the board with an old knife or palette knife. Make sure the board is completely covered, but don't apply too much adhesive or it will ooze up between the tiles.*

4 *Lay the tiles on the adhesive in your desired pattern. Most mosaic tiles are ridged on one side and should be laid ridged side down. Remember to leave ⅟₁₆in (2mm) between each one. Leave the tiles to dry overnight.*

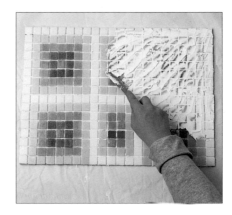

5 *Spread some ready-mixed grouting over the tiles with the knife. Spread it diagonally across, allowing it to sink into the spaces between the tiles. Try to make sure that all of the gaps are well filled.*

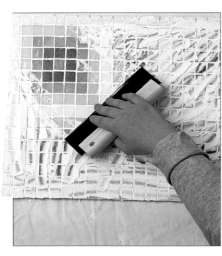

6 *Draw the squeegy tool firmly over the tiles, removing excess grouting from the surface and pressing grouting down between the tiles. You will need to stop from time to time and wipe excess grouting off the tool. Once the surface is reasonably clear, check that there is enough grouting between the tiles. Add more if necessary.*

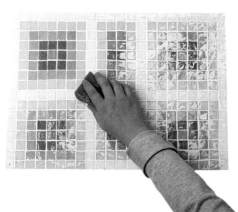

7 *Take an old damp sponge and wipe any grouting off the tiles. Leave to dry thoroughly and then buff with a dry cloth to remove any powdery deposits.*

WINDOW SHADE

Simple to make and hang • Provides privacy • Easy to raise and lower

WITH A SIMPLE cord mechanism based on slatted bamboo blinds, this shade is made of two layers of coordinating fabric. It is attached to a covered lath with touch-and-close tape. Two screw eyes are set in the lath behind the shade and the ends of two cords are tied securely to them. The cords run down the back of the shade, around the wooden dowel that is slotted into the bottom, and up the front of the shade. They then thread through rings that have been attached to the top of the shade with small fabric ties. The cords are pulled to the side to be secured on a cleat. When the cords are pulled, the shade rolls smoothly up and down. Allow enough length so that even when the shade is lowered, there is still some fabric rolled up to show off the lining.

Choosing fabric *Choose fabrics of compatible weight. Sturdy sailcloth and ticking are a good combination and lend themselves to bathrooms with a seaside or nautical theme.*

PROJECT PLANNER

3 HOURS

Tools and Materials
Main fabric: width of finished shade, plus 1¼in (3cm) x length of window, plus 6in (15cm) (see p.129)
• Lining fabric: as main fabric and for two ties with finished size of ⅝ x 7in (1.5 x 18cm)
• Touch-and-close tape • Dowel (slightly under finished width) • Two rings • Two lengths of cord:
one 3 x length of the shade plus width of shade, and one 3 x length of shade • Two screw eyes
• Toggle • Wall cleat • One 1 x 2in (2.5 x 5cm) batten • Sewing machine and thread to match fabric

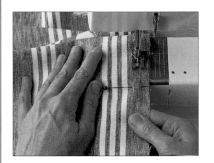

1 *Place main fabric and lining right sides together and pin. Machine stitch side seams, making a ⅝in (1.5cm) seam allowance.*

2 *Turn the shade right side out and press the sides flat. At the base of the shade, press ⅜in (1cm) to the right side and then 2¼in (3cm) and pin. Machine stitch close to top folded edge to form the slot for the dowel. Press.*

3 *At the top of the shade, press over ⅜in (1cm) to the back of the shade and pin. Lay a length of touch-and-close tape (soft side) over the hem, just down from the top edge of the shade. Machine stitch top and bottom, holding it in place as you sew.*

4 *Insert the dowel into the casing at the base of the shade. Finish the ends of the casing with slipstitch (see p.138).*

5 *Make two straight ties (see p.146) each measuring ⅝ x 7in (1.5 x 18cm). Thread a ring onto each tie. Cover the batten and attach hard side of touch-and-close (see p.144).*

6 *Attach shade to the batten with the touch-and-close. Fold a tie in half and position on the batten about 15cm (6in) from the end of the shade and overlapping the shade by about 1in (2.5cm). Staple it in position. Staple the second tie 6in (15cm) from the other end.*

7 *Roll up the shade. Insert screw eyes on the underside of the batten, 6in (15cm) from each end as for ties. Take the two lengths of cord and knot the longer cord to the screw eye on the left and the shorter cord to the one on the right. Thread as shown right.*

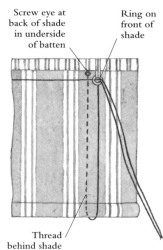

Screw eye at back of shade in underside of batten

Ring on front of shade

Thread behind shade

FROSTED GLASS PANEL

Decorative • Simple to do • Creates a stylish screen

THE DELICATE, translucent look of real frosted or etched glass can be easily achieved with the help of frosting spray and is a perfect way to add decorative interest to a glass-paneled door. Cutout shapes are placed on the glass before spraying the frosting. When they are removed, the unfrosted areas of glass beneath are revealed, creating an attractive pattern. If the shapes are kept reasonably small, the frosting also provides some privacy. Always wear a face mask and keep windows open when using any kind of spray product.

A subtle screen *Sea creatures and fronds of seaweed strike a jaunty marine note on this bathroom door. The snowy frosting creates a subtle screen and is a simple way to provide some privacy.*

PROJECT PLANNER

2 HOURS

Tools and Materials
Frosting spray • Face mask • Cutout shapes or reverse stencils • Mounting spray glue • Newspaper • Masking tape • Glass cleaner

1 *Use the shapes on p. 185 or designs of your choice to make the masking shapes. Take some sheets of newspaper and, using masking tape, stick them all around the pane of glass to protect the woodwork and walls. Be careful to tape the paper right at the edge of the pane so no glass is covered by newspaper. Make sure the glass is clean and dry.*

2 *Decide how you want to place your shapes. Spray the back of a shape with mounting spray and place carefully on the glass. Repeat with all of the shapes to make the desired design (see inset).*

3 *Apply the frosting spray all over the glass panel, making sure the coverage is as even as possible. Wear a mask when using the spray, and make sure the room is well ventilated. Let the frosting spray dry for about 15 minutes.*

4 *Carefully peel off the shapes to reveal the unfrosted areas beneath. Leave for about half an hour and then wipe off any remaining glue with glass cleaner.*

SEWING TECHNIQUES

EQUIPMENT

The home furnishing projects in this book do not call for a lot of sophisticated equipment. For most, a sewing machine is essential, and it is useful, but not vital, to have a model that can do zigzag stitching and buttonholes. Always have an iron close at hand – seam and hem allowances need to be pressed in place. Other basic items include good sharp scissors for cutting fabric, plus smaller scissors for other tasks. A fabric tape measure is useful for measuring small areas such as hems, but you might also like to have a wooden yardstick for measuring larger areas on your work surface.

Sewing

Pins, needles, and thread

Pins, needles, and thread are essential items for any sewing box. Plain pins are fine, but pins with colored heads are easier to find and remove from large swathes of fabric. A pincushion is a useful way of making sure pins stay in the right place. Sewing thread can be used for basting and for hand and machine sewing.

Sewing machine

If possible, your sewing machine should have a zigzag facility, a zipper foot, and a buttonhole foot for the projects in this book.

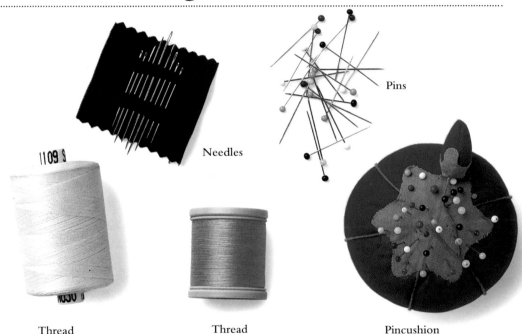

Needles

Pins

Thread

Thread

Pincushion

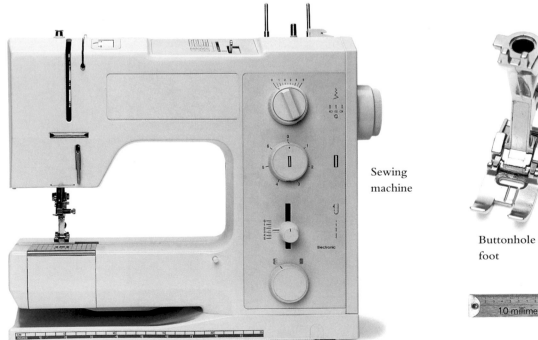

Sewing machine

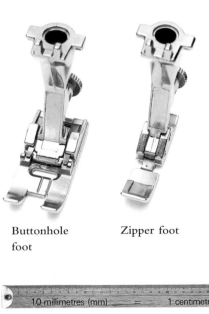

Buttonhole foot

Zipper foot

Measuring, Cutting, and Pressing

Cutting tools

A pair of good-quality dressmaker's scissors will make all the difference to your sewing projects, enabling you to cut fabric efficiently. Never use your fabric scissors on paper – it will dull the blades. Pinking shears are useful for finishing the raw edges of seams (see p.133), and you will also need smaller scissors for tasks such as clipping seams. A stitch ripper is better than scissors for removing stitching from fabric.

Markers and measurers

Tailor's chalk is ideal for marking fabric because it dusts off easily. You may also need pencils and markers for making templates. A tape measure is essential – never guess the measurements of a project.

Iron

A steam iron and ironing board should always be on hand for pressing fabrics.

Dressmaker's scissors

Stitch ripper

Embroidery scissors

Small sewing scissors

Pinking shears

Pencil

Iron

Water-soluble marker

Tailor's chalk

Tape measure

| 100 centimetres (cm) | = | 1 metre (m) | 1000 metres (m) | = | 1 kilometre (km) |

Wooden yardstick

MEASURING AND ESTIMATING

Always measure and estimate fabric requirements accurately before starting projects. For draperies, curtains, and shades, take two basic measurements – the "finished width" and the "finished length." To calculate the "working width"(the width to cut), add an allowance for fullness to the finished width. To calculate the "working length" (the length to cut), add an allowance for hems and headings to the finished length. If using a patterned fabric, add an allowance for matching the pattern (see page opposite). For curtains, it is best to install the track or pole from which they will hang before you start. As a rule, tracks and poles are usually mounted 4–6in (10–15cm) above the window frame and extend 6–8in (15–20cm) each side, as space permits, to allow room for the curtains when drawn back.

Measuring a Window for Curtains

Once your track or pole is up, measure the width first, then the length. Jot your measurements down as soon as you have taken them to avoid getting them wrong. It is essential to use an extendable metal tape measure; a fabric measure will give inaccurate measurements.

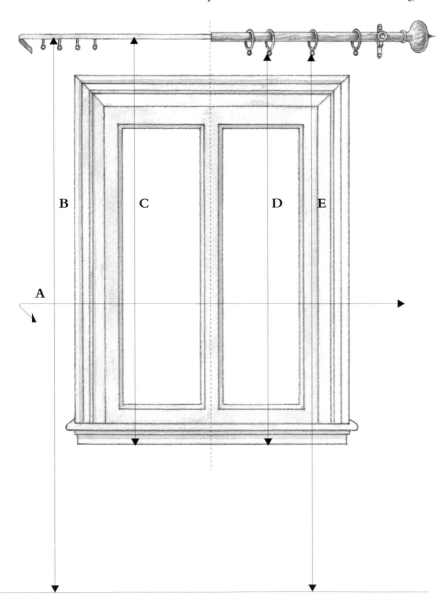

Finished width Measure the entire span of the track or pole (**A**). If the track projects out from the wall, include the return (the distance it projects from the wall) at both ends in your measurement. If the track has an overlap arm that meets in the center, add the amount of overlap to the width.

Finished length Use the top of the track (**B** and **C**), or the bottom of the curtain rings on a pole (**D** and **E**) as the starting point for your finished length measurement. (For slot-, tie-, or tab-headed curtains measure from the pole top). Measure down to the sill (**C** and **D**) or floor (**B** and **E**). Subtract ½in (1cm) if you want curtains to clear the floor, or add 1in (2.5cm) if you want them on the floor.

To estimate the amount of fabric Decide how much fullness you want for your curtains: 1½ times the width for flat or tab headed curtains; 2 or 2½ times the width for gathered or pleated headings. Multiply the finished width measurement by the amount of fullness you want to find your working width. Divide the working width by the width of your fabric and round the answer up to the next whole number to get the number of widths or "drops" you will need. For a pair of curtains, divide this by 2 for the number of widths in each curtain. Add up to 12in (30cm) for hem and heading allowance to the finished length measurement to get your working length. If there is a pattern repeat, allow extra for that (see page opposite).

Multiply the working length measurement by the number of drops required to calculate your overall fabric requirement.

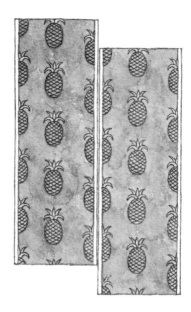

Estimating extra fabric for pattern repeats

Once you have the working length, measure the length of a complete pattern on your fabric. Divide the working length by the pattern length. Round this up to the next whole number and multiply by the pattern length. This will give you the amount of fabric you need to cut to match the pattern across widths.

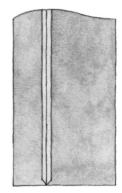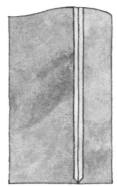

Joining widths and half widths

If a pair of curtains requires three widths, cut one width in half and make each curtain of one and a half widths. Place the half width at the outside of the curtain and the full width in the center.

Measuring a Window for a Shade

A shade is usually attached to a wooden batten, usually 1 x 2in (2.5 x 5cm) softwood cut to the finished width of the shade. Before you start, decide where the batten is to be mounted – to the wall above the window, to the top of the window frame (or architrave), or, if the window is recessed, to the inside of the recess.

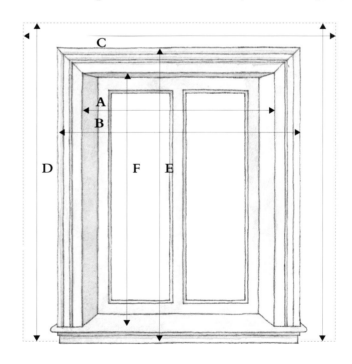

Finished width Measure the width of the area you wish the shade to cover – either the width of the recess (**A**), the width of the architrave (**B**), or wider if you want the shade to extend to either side of the window frame (**C**). For a recessed window, to make sure the shade moves freely up and down, deduct ¾in (2cm) from the width of the recess.

Finished length This is usually dictated by where the shade is mounted in the window area. If the shade is hanging from the wall above the window, it should drop to just below the sill (**D**); if it is attached to the frame, it should drop to the sill, or just below it (**E**); and if it is mounted inside the recess, it can only drop to the sill (**F**). Some shades need extra length for fullness when they are down (see Shade with Ties p.14).

Working measurements For the working width of a shade, add two side hem allowances to the finished width measurement. Allow 2in (5cm) for each or see individual project. For the working length, add a hem and a heading allowance to the finished length measurement. Allow 2in (5cm) for each or see individual project. It is best to allow at least 2in (5cm) extra at the top of the shade. This allows room for error and any excess can be trimmed off before finishing the heading.

Estimating fabric Divide the working width by the width of your fabric. If the answer is less than one, you will only need one width of fabric and the total length of fabric required is the working length. If the answer is more than one, you will have to join widths of fabric to get the full working width of the shade. The extra width is usually divided in two and joined to each side of the first width so there is a central panel and two joining seams. To calculate the amount of fabric you need, multiply the number of widths required by the working length (plus any extra required to match a pattern, see above).

129

Measuring a Pillow Form

When making several pillow covers, it is worth making a paper
pattern of the pillow form first. Do not add seam allowances so the covers will fit snugly,
making the finished pillows look pleasingly plump.

For a conventional cover with a top and bottom
piece, simply measure the width and length of
the pad. For an envelope cover, measure the
width, but allow twice the length plus about 8in
(20cm) for the envelope flap.

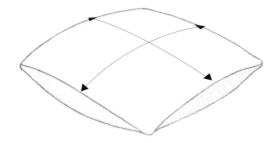

Measuring a Bolster

A standard bolster pillow is 18in (46cm) long, with a diameter of 7in (18cm).
The simplest method of covering a bolster is to make a long cover that ties at each end
like a Christmas present and extends into a ruffle.

Measure the circumference and length of the
bolster and across each end for the diameter. For
a cover without a separate end piece, measure
from the center of one end, down the length to
the center of the other end. Add to this
measurement enough extra length to gather the
fabric together and form a gathered end. Add
seam allowances of ⅝in (1.5cm) all around.

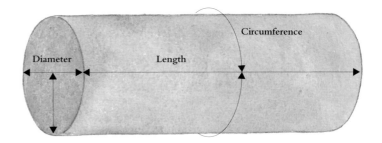

Measuring a Box Cushion

A conventional box cushion has a top and bottom piece, and a "stand" (or
depth) that runs all around the sides of the cushion. A simple method of covering a box cushion
is to make a flat cover and miter the corners to make a box shape.

In this simple method of covering a box
cushion, the flat cover has to include the
"stand" or depth measurement as well as the
length and width. Measure the length of the
cushion and add one depth measurement. Then
measure the width of the cushion, double that,
and add twice the depth of the pad. Finally add
seam allowances of ⅝in (1.5cm) all around.

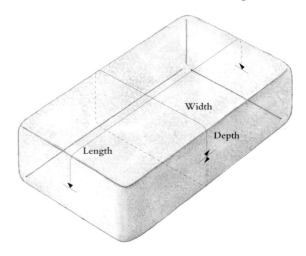

Measuring a Chair

A squab cushion should fit a chair seat neatly, so start by
making a paper pattern of the seat area. Place the paper on the chair seat
and trace around the shape with a pencil.

Measure the length and width of the chair seat.
Make the pattern on the generous side so the
edges of the paper extend slightly beyond the
edges of the chair. Once the pad is covered
with jersey and the tight-fitting cover, it will be
slightly smaller than the original pattern, and a
cushion that is too small for the seat looks
mean and uncomfortable. Mark where the
chair struts extend from the seat so you will
know where to attach ties to the cover.

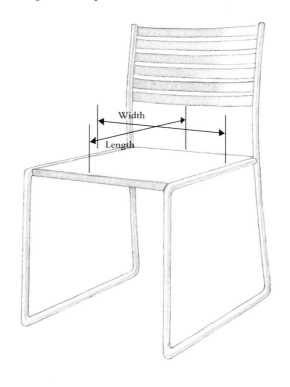

Measuring a Table

For a rectangular tablecloth, first decide on how much overhang you want.
Sit at a chair and measure from the top of the table to just above your lap. Alternatively, you may
want to make a longer cloth that reaches to the floor.

Measure the length and
width of the tabletop. Add
twice your desired overhang
measurement to both the
length and the width of the
tabletop and then add seam
allowances all around to
obtain the overall dimensions
of the cloth. If you are
adding a border to the tablecloth, subtract the depth of
the border from the overall
width and length measure-
ment. For a border, cut
fabric twice the finished
depth plus seam allowances.

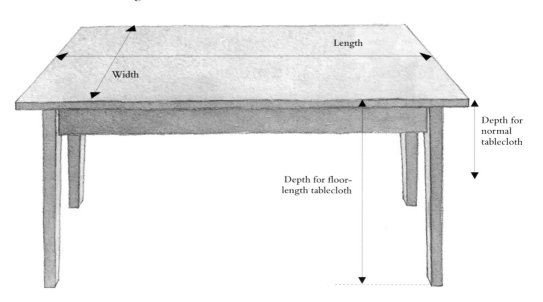

CUTTING AND STITCHING

Before you start any home furnishing project, make sure you have everything you need in terms of equipment and that your sewing machine is in good working order. Take exact measurements – whether of windows, pillow forms, or furniture – very carefully and always double-check them before you start to cut fabric.

When cutting, use really sharp scissors. A pair of good-quality dressmaker's scissors will last for years and make your task much easier. None of the projects in this book is difficult, but a little attention to detail before you start will make all the difference and help you achieve a satisfying and professional-looking result.

Cutting on the Grain

Fabric is usually cut directly down or across the material on the horizontal or vertical grain. It is particularly important that curtains and shades are cut absolutely square or they will not hang correctly.

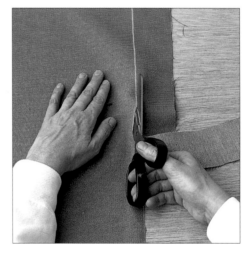

1 *To make sure you have a straight edge at right angles to the selvage, place the fabric flat on a table, with the selvage aligned along one side. Let the fabric hang slightly over the edge of the table. Draw a line with tailor's chalk along the table edge to mark the straight grain as shown.*

2 *Place the fabric on the table and cut along the chalked line, keeping as straight as possible. Work from this straight edge when measuring and cutting the fabric. Use sharp scissors, preferably with long blades.*

Cutting on the Bias

Fabric cut on the bias molds around curves and corners more easily, so use bias-cut fabric for ties that are to be tied into bows and for piping and cording to fit around shapes.

1 *Fold in a corner of a width of fabric at a right angle. Check that the angle is correct by aligning the fabric with a piece of paper as shown. Press to mark the fold line.*

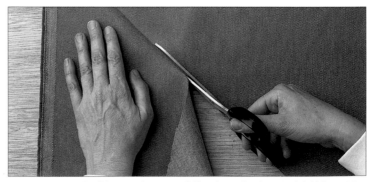

2 *Open out the fabric and cut carefully along the diagonal fold line. Use sharp scissors and keep the cut as straight as possible.*

Sewing a Flat Seam

A flat seam is the simplest way to join two pieces of fabric. To keep seam allowances even and seams straight, align the raw edges of the fabric to the appropriate seam guidelines on your sewing machine.

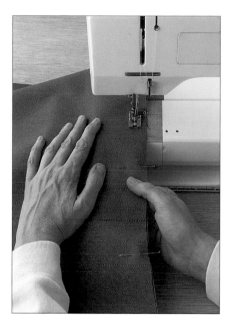

1 *With right sides together, pin the fabric with raw edges together. Machine stitch, making a ⅝in (1.5cm) seam allowance. Backstitch at the start and finish of the stitching to reinforce the seam.*

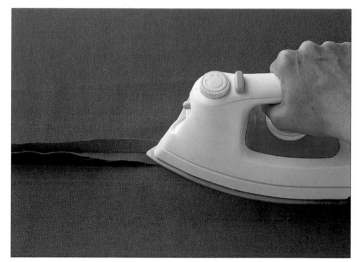

2 *Open out the fabric and place right side down on an ironing board or a flat surface suitable for ironing upon. Using the tip of the iron, press the seam flat.*

Finishing Raw Edges

The raw edges of a flat seam may need to be finished in some way to minimize fraying, particularly if the seam will be subject to strain or frequent washing. Here are two methods.

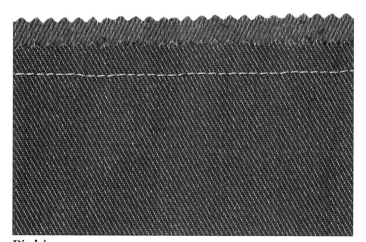

Pinking

Trim the raw edges of the seam with pinking shears to reduce fraying. To reduce bulk when using thick fabric, you can trim one side closer to the line of stitching than the other.

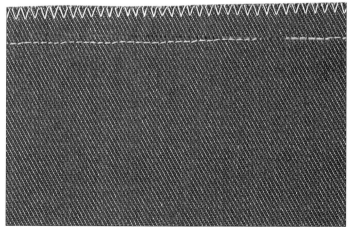

Zigzag stitching

Set the zigzag stitch on your machine to medium. Machine stitch along the seam allowance, stitching close to but not on the raw edges. You can stitch both edges together as here or zigzag single layers.

French Seam

This is an enclosed seam in which the raw edges are
sewn into the finished seam. It creates a neat finish, which is particularly
useful for unlined items such as curtains or bedspreads.

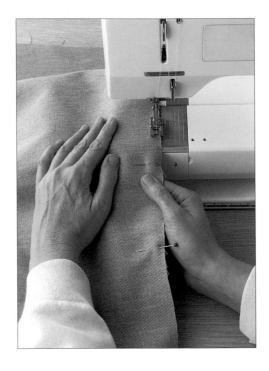

1 *With wrong
sides together,
pin the pieces of
fabric together and
machine stitch
¼in (5mm) from
the raw edges.*

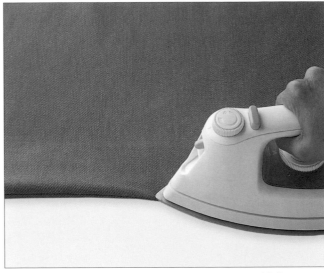

2 *Open out the fabric and press the seam open. Fold the
fabric right sides together and press so the seam is exactly
on the folded edge.*

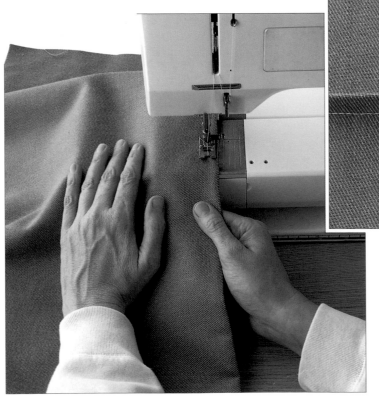

3 *On the wrong side, machine stitch ½in (1cm) from the fold
line. When the seam is completed, the raw edges are neatly
enclosed on the wrong side (see inset). Press the seam to one side
on the wrong side so it lies flat.*

Satin Stitch

A decorative machine stitch used for applying appliqué or for
effect. Practice on a scrap of fabric before trying satin stitch on your finished work.
You need a swing-needle machine with a zigzag facility for this stitch.

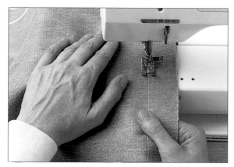

1 *With the stitch length set on long, do a guideline of machine stitching to follow. (For appliqué, simply follow the line of the piece of fabric you are attaching.) Set your machine to satin stitch, with a medium stitch width and the stitch length just above zero. Align the center of the presser foot with the guideline and satin stitch along the line.*

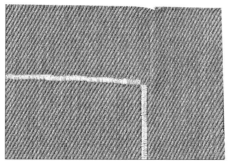

2 *To satin stitch around a corner, stop when you reach the corner, lift the foot, and pivot the work 90 degrees. Put the foot back down and continue stitching.*

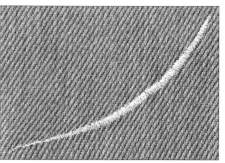

3 *For tapering satin stitch (useful in appliqué), start with the stitch length set just below zero and the stitch width at zero. Hold the work steady with your left hand, keeping the right hand free to adjust the stitch width. Start stitching and gradually adjust the stitch width control slowly and smoothly up to a medium width in the center of the piece of stitching and back down to zero again at the end.*

How to Keep Machine Stitching Straight

When you are stitching farther than usual from the edge of the
fabric, place a piece of masking tape on the machine to help you align the fabric
and keep your line of stitching perfectly straight.

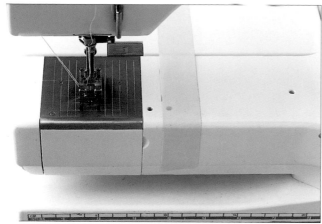

1 *Measure the distance between the line you are going to stitch and the edge of the fabric. Measure this same distance from the needle out to the right and mark with a piece of masking tape.*

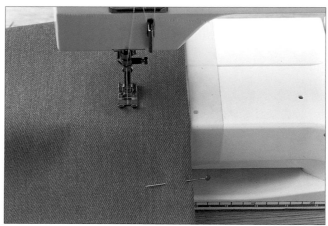

2 *Place the fabric so the edge aligns with the inside of the masking tape. This will help you keep your line of machine stitching straight.*

Blunting Corners

A blunted corner creates a well-defined point when the fabric is
turned right side out. Make one diagonal stitch across the corner for fine fabric, two
for medium-weight fabric, and three or four for heavyweight fabric.

1 *Machine stitch to the corner, stopping just short of it. Lift the machine foot and pivot fabric on the needle. Drop the foot and stitch diagonally across the corner. Lift the foot to pivot the fabric before lowering and stitching along next side.*

2 *To reduce bulk at the corner, trim away the seam allowance across the point, close to the stitching. Then taper it on each side. Fabric that frays easily should not be trimmed too close to the seam.*

Snipping into Corners

Snipping into a corner allows you to maneuver a straight piece of fabric
around a corner. This technique is used when attaching a boxing strip to a flat section, for example, or
when attaching piping or cording around the corner of a cushion cover.

1 *Machine stitch toward the corner, stopping about 1in (2.5cm) before it. Mark the seamline with chalk and clip the seam allowance ⅝in (1.5cm) from the corner.*

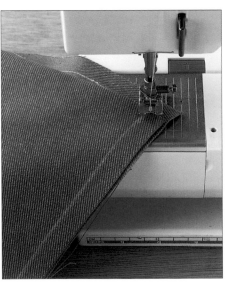

2 *Stitch to the corner and lift the foot. Spread the clipped section so the straight edge fits around the corner. Pivot the work on the needle so the foot faces in the direction of the next line of stitching.*

3 *Lower the foot and continue machine stitching in the new direction.*

Box Cushion Corners

A quick and simple way to make a box cushion is to start
with a flat cushion and miter the corners to create the necessary depth or "stand."
The kitchen bench cushion (see p.68) is made in this way.

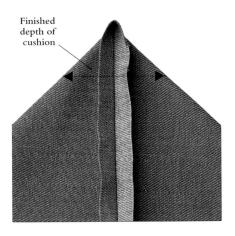

Finished
depth of
cushion

1 *Having stitched the side seam of the cushion, place the fabric so the corner forms a point and the side seam is centered on this point. Using tailor's chalk, mark a line across the corner that corresponds to the finished depth of the cushion.*

2 *Machine stitch along this chalk line. Backstitch at the start and finish of the stitching to secure.*

3 *Trim off the corner beyond the line of machine stitching about ½in (1cm) above the chalked line. Repeat Steps 1–3 at the other corners.*

4 *Turn the cover right side out. The finished corner gives the cushion the necessary depth.*

Mitering Corners

Use this technique to make neat corners on square
or rectangular items, such as curtain hems. It is also useful for
smaller items such as table napkins.

1 *Fold over the hem allowances and press to make crease lines. Unfold the hem allowances and fold in the corner at right angles so the center of the new fold is at the point where the crease lines meet.*

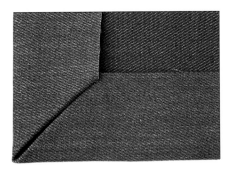

2 *Fold in the hem allowances again so they meet neatly at the corner as shown.*

HAND STITCHES

Most of the stitching in the home furnishing projects in this book is done by machine, but some stages must be stitched by hand. Unless the stitching is temporary, always start and finish your stitching securely. Start with a knot, which can be hidden on the wrong side or inside a hem. Finish with several backstitches worked over one another.

The following instructions are worked for a right-handed stitcher. Reverse the direction if you are left-handed.

Running Stitch

This is a short, even stitch that is used for gathering a length of fabric, such as a ruffled border around a pillow cover.

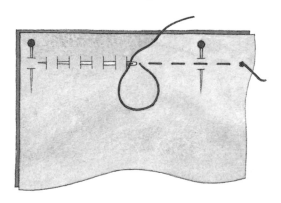

Secure thread with a knot. Working from right to left, weave the needle in and out of the fabric several times before pulling it through.

Basting Stitch

A longer version of running stitch, basting is used to hold two or more layers of fabric together temporarily.

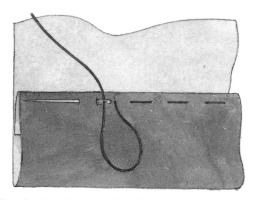

Secure thread with a knot. Working from right to left, make a series of straight stitches each about ⅝in (1.5cm) long.

Even Slipstitch

This is a nearly invisible stitch that you use to join two folded edges together.

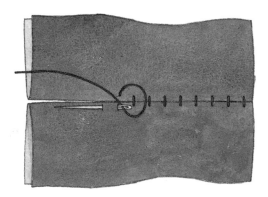

Working from right to left, come up through one folded edge and make a stitch about ¼in (5mm) long through the opposite folded edge. Pull the thread through. Continue this way, taking alternate stitches on each folded edge.

Uneven Slipstitch

This is a nearly invisible hemming technique that you use to join a folded edge to a flat surface.

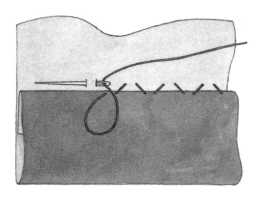

Working from right to left, come up through the folded edge of the hem. Make a small stitch in the flat fabric catching only a few threads. Take a ½in (1cm) running stitch through the opposite folded edge. Repeat to the end, alternating small and larger running stitches on the flat fabric and folded edge.

Couching Stitch

Use this stitch to attach rings or curtain hooks to fabric. It is best to use double thread to give extra strength.

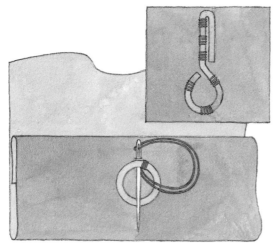

Using double thread, secure the thread in the fabric and make a simple stitch over and over in the same place until the ring is firmly attached. To attach a hook, make several groups of stitches all around the hook.

Herringbone

A neat stitch, this is useful for curtain hems. It is generally worked from left to right, but left-handed people should work from right to left.

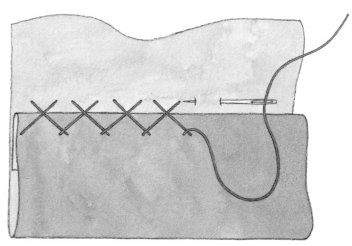

Work from left to right. Secure the thread and bring the needle through the hem. With needle pointing left, take a small stitch in the fabric above the hem edge and about 1in (2.5cm) to the right. Take the next stitch in the hem edge, again about 1in (2.5cm) to the right with the needle pointing left. Repeat, alternating stitches as shown.

French Knot

A decorative embroidery stitch, this forms a neat knot on the surface of the work, which is perfect for adding texture. Use six-ply embroidery floss and an embroidery needle.

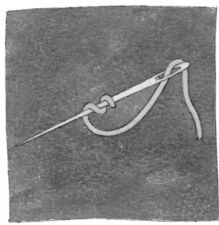

1 *Secure the thread in the fabric and bring the needle through to the right side. Twist the needle two or three times around the thread, depending on how big you want the knot to be.*

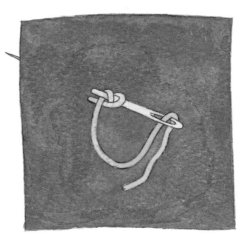

2 *Insert the needle back into the fabric near the starting point and pull the thread through to the wrong side to make the knot. Secure the thread on the wrong side.*

CURTAINS AND SHADES

When working with the large expanses of fabric needed for curtains, it is best to have a work surface where you can spread the fabric out flat. This will help you make sure you cut the fabric absolutely straight so the finished item hangs correctly. Always double-check your measurements before you start assembling the project – there is nothing worse than finding your carefully stitched curtain or shade is too short for the window.

Making a Basic Curtain

Cut lining 4in (10cm) longer than the finished length and 1½in (4cm) narrower than the finished width (before pleating or gathering). See page 128 for information on how to measure a window and estimate fabric.

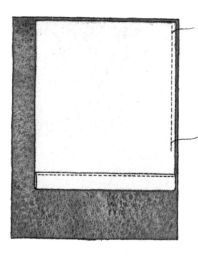

1 *Turn over a 2in (5cm) double hem on the lining and press. Machine stitch the hem in place. With right sides together and the top and one side edge aligned, pin lining to the main fabric, ⅝in (1.5cm) from top of curtain down to about 4in (10cm) above the lining hem. Machine stitch and press seam toward the lining.*

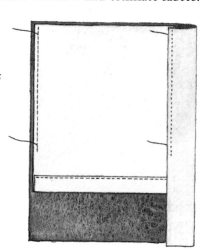

2 *Pull the lining over to align with the other side of the curtain fabric. Pin the sides together. Machine stitch the lining and main fabric together, making a ⅝in (1.5cm) seam allowance, down to about 4in (10cm) above the lining hem. Press seam toward the lining.*

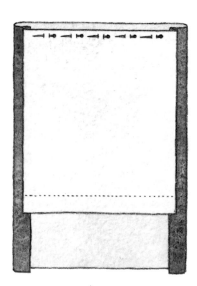

3 *Turn the curtain right side out and center the lining so the curtain side hems are both the same width – 1½in (3.5cm). Pin across the top of curtain and lining to hold them in place.*

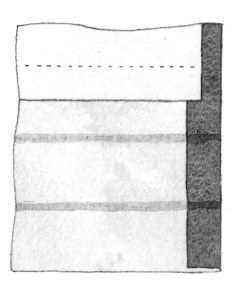

4 *Fold over 8in (20cm) at the base of the curtain fabric and press. Open the fabric out and fold the raw edge up to meet the 8in (20cm) fold line. Press.*

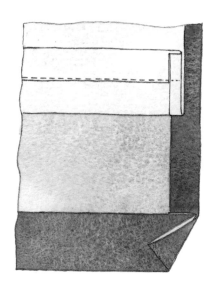

5 *Fold the hem up along the lower fold line. Miter the corner of curtain by turning corner in diagonally 2in (5cm).*

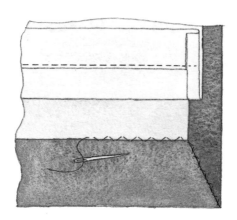

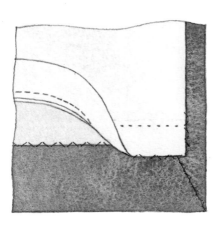

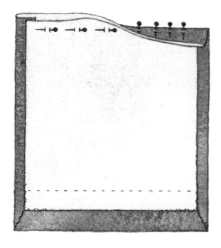

6 *Fold hem over again along the upper fold line. Sew miters and hem in place by hand, using even slipstitch (see p. 138).*

7 *Slipstitch the lining to the curtain from the end of the machine stitching and 2in (5cm) around corner. Finish securely. Repeat at the opposite corner.*

8 *Measure up from base of curtain several times across the width and mark the finished length along the top of the curtain with pins. Fold top of curtain down along pinned line and press. Remove horizontal pins and repin vertically to hold fold.*

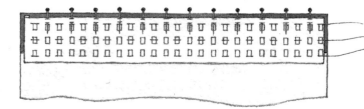

9 *Take a length of curtain tape and knot the strings together at the leading end of tape. Fold the tape under ⅝ in (1.5cm). Pin the tape level with the top of the curtain, aligning the folded end with leading edge. At the other end of tape, pull strings free and fold under the end of the tape ⅝ in (1.5cm) so the folded edge is aligned with the edge of the curtain.*

10 *Start machine stitching at the top left-hand corner of tape. Backstitch to secure at the beginning, then stitch along the top of the tape close to the edge. Backstitch at the end. Stitch the bottom of the tape to the curtain the same way.*

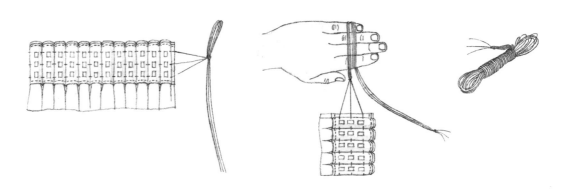

11 *Pull up the curtain strings until the gathered width equals the width of your pole or track (do not forget returns and overlaps). Knot the strings with a slip knot, pulling the loop of the knot through about 3in (7.5cm). To keep the strings neat, make a roll by putting your fingers through the loop and winding the rest of the strings around them. Tuck the roll under the strings in the fold of a pleat on the tape.*

141

Attaching Touch-and-Close Tape to a Valance

A valance shelf should be between 4 and 8in (10–20cm) deep,
depending on the fullness of the draperies hung below. It is mounted on the wall
above the window with right-angled shelf brackets.

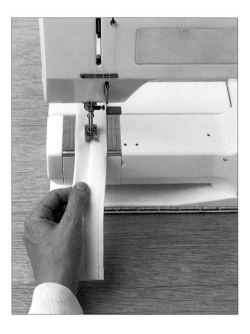

2 *Take the soft side of the touch-and-close tape and machine stitch to the top half of the right side of the lining strip, staying close to the top edge. Stitch the bottom edge of the touch-and-close and trim off any excess at the end.*

1 *Take a strip of lining fabric, measuring the length of the finished valance (including returns) plus 1¼in (3cm), by the depth of the curtain tape plus 1¼in (3cm). Turn over ⅝in (1.5cm) at the top and bottom edges of the strip and press. Turn under ⅝in (1.5cm) at each end and press.*

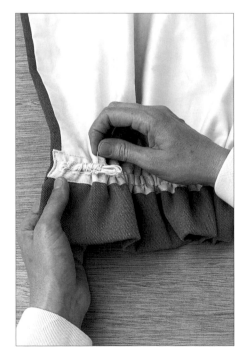

3 *Pull up the threads on the valance tape to gather it to the required width, making sure the gathers are evenly spaced. Make a slip knot in the threads and wind them into a neat bundle. Stitch the bundle to the tape.*

4 *Using slipstitch (see p.138), hand sew the lining strip with the touch-and-close facing outward over the gathered tape. Stitch top and bottom, working over the gathers.*

5 *Staple the hard side of the touch-and-close tape to the front and side edges of the valance shelf.*

Attaching Touch-and-Close Tape to the Top of a Shade

A roman shade can be attached to a supporting batten with touch-and-close tape.
The soft side of a touch-and-close strip is sewn to the top of the shade. The hard side is stapled
to a batten, which is then screwed on or above the window frame.

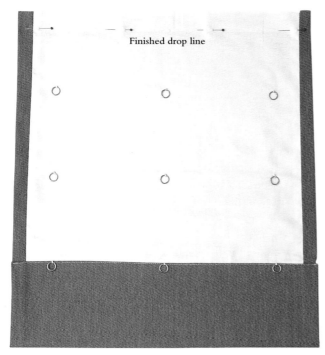

1 *Measure the finished drop from the base of the shade and mark with a line of pins. Fold over at the marked line and press.*

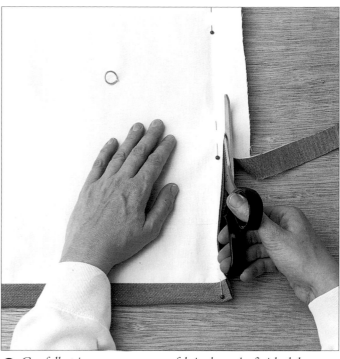

2 *Carefully trim away any excess fabric above the finished drop line, leaving a hem of about ½in (1cm).*

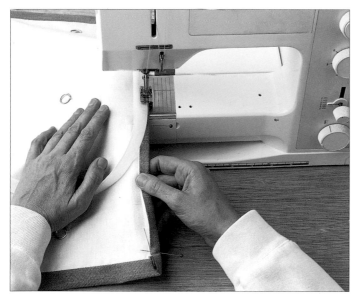

3 *Machine stitch the soft side of the touch-and-close tape over the top hem. Keep very close to the top folded edge of the hem and remove pins as you reach them. Backstitch at the start and finish of the line of machine stitching.*

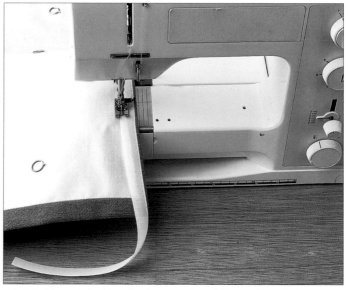

4 *Machine stitch along the bottom edge of the touch-and-close, backstitching at the start and finish as before. Trim off any excess touch-and-close.*

Covering a Batten for a Shade

For a neat coordinated finish, the batten for a shade should be wrapped in a strip of
the shade fabric before attaching touch-and-close tape and screw eyes. The batten can then be
mounted on the wall or window frame using 1½in (4cm) right-angle brackets.

1 *Use a piece of standard 1 x 2in (2.5 x 5cm) wooden batten the width of the shade. Cut a length of fabric 6in (15cm) wide by the length of the batten plus 2in (5cm). Wrap the fabric around the wood and staple one side. Wrap the other side around and staple it in place.*

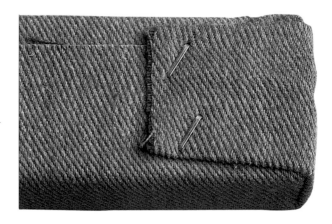

2 *Fold the ends over neatly as though wrapping a package and staple in place. If the fabric is thick, cut away some of the excess fabric underneath before stapling.*

3 *Using a staple gun, staple the hard side of the touch-and-close tape to the front edge of the batten. Insert enough staples to hold the touch-and-close securely.*

4 *Position screw eyes in line with the cords on the shade and ⅝in (1.5cm) from the front edge. Position an extra screw eye ¾in (2cm) from the end of the batten at the side where the cords will hang down – usually the right. Use an awl to make a hole through the fabric and into the wood, and then insert screw eyes.*

Cording a Shade

A roman shade is raised and lowered by a system of cords.
The cords run through vertical rows of rings sewn to the back of the
shade and then through screw eyes on the shade batten.

There are usually three cords on a roman shade running through three rows of rings. One row is set 4in (10cm) in from the right-hand edge of the shade, another is 4in (10cm) from the left-hand edge of the shade and the third runs up the center. A screw eye is mounted on the underside of the batten above each row of rings and an extra screw eye is placed ¾in (2cm) from the end of the batten at the side where the cords will hang down. If the shade is wider than about 48in (120cm), you might want to add another row of rings so there are four cords.

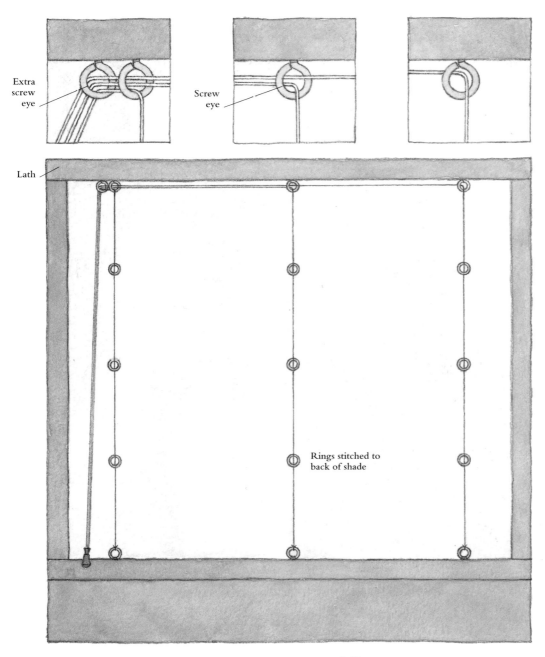

Extra screw eye

Screw eye

Lath

Rings stitched to back of shade

1 Cut three lengths of cord, each roughly 2½ times the length of the shade. String up the shade by tying a cord to each of the bottom rings and threading it through all the rings above it.

2 Attach the shade to the batten (see p.143) and pass each cord through the screw eye directly above it and across through the other screw eyes, including the extra one at the end of the batten.

3 Thread all the cord ends through a cord weight and check that the shade is pulling up level. Knot the cords together below the weight and cut off any surplus. Attach a cleat or hook to the wall or window frame. When the shade is raised, wind the cords around the cleat to hold it.

FINISHING TECHNIQUES

Small details, such as neatly made buttonholes on a pillow cover, bias-cut piping around a headboard, or a matching stiffened tieback on a curtain, can make all the difference to homemade furnishings. These simple but effective finishing techniques all feature in the projects, but are also useful for other items you might wish to make. Don't be tempted to rush these final touches – that little bit of extra effort is sure to pay off.

Straight Tie

Ties made from fabric cut on the straight grain of fabric are ideal where the tie does not need to be very flexible. This style could be used for the loosely knotted ties that hold a shade or fasten a pillow cover.

1 *Cut a piece of fabric twice the width of the finished tie plus ½in (1cm) seam allowance. Press ¼in (5mm) to the wrong side along each long side of the fabric.*

2 *Fold the tie in half lengthwise with the folded edges together and press.*

3 *At one end of the tie, fold in the raw edges ¼in (5mm). Machine stitch across this end and along the long side, keeping close to the folded edge. Leave the other end open. The raw edges will be concealed when the tie is attached to the item.*

Stitching on a Tie

This method of attaching a tie with a rectangle of stitching means that it is firmly secured. The method can be used to attach straight or bias-cut ties or ties made from tape or ribbon.

1 *Tuck under the raw edges of the tie and pin it in position. Start machine stitching at the top left corner, backstitching to secure. Stitch down the left side of the tie, counting stitches so you can make the same number on the other side. With the needle in the work, lift the foot and pivot the work. Lower the foot.*

2 *Machine stitch along the bottom of the rectangle. Lift the foot and pivot the work again. Lower the foot.*

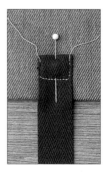

3 *Machine stitch up the right-hand side of the rectangle, checking that you make the same number of stitches as on the left side. Pivot the work again.*

4 *Machine stitch across the top of the rectangle.*

5 *Machine stitch diagonally across the rectangle from top left to bottom right. Finally stitch up the right-hand side again to secure.*

Cutting and Joining Bias Strips

Fabric cut on the bias instead of the straight grain
has more "give," so use bias-cut strips to cover piping cord and to make
ties that require flexibility.

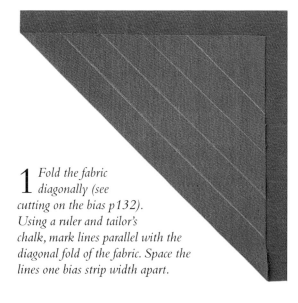

1 *Fold the fabric
diagonally (see
cutting on the bias p132).
Using a ruler and tailor's
chalk, mark lines parallel with the
diagonal fold of the fabric. Space the
lines one bias strip width apart.*

2 *Cut along the
folded diagonal line
and along all the
subsequent chalk lines.
Use sharp scissors and
cut the fabric as straight
as possible.*

3 *To join the strips, pin the ends of two strips with
right sides together so they form a right angle.
Machine stitch ½in (1cm) from the ends.*

4 *Press the seam
open. To finish
the bias strips, trim
off excess fabric from
the corners.*

Bias-cut Tie

Fabric cut on the bias is more flexible. Ties made from
bias-cut strips will therefore tie into bows more easily than straight ties.
The length and width of the ties will depend on the project.

1 *Cut a bias strip to twice the width of the finished tie
plus 1¼in (3cm). Fold the strip in half lengthwise
with right sides together. Machine stitch ⅝in (1.5cm)
from the raw edges. Backstitch at the start and finish of
the stitching to secure.*

2 *Carefully trim the seam allowance to about ¼in (5mm) or less from the line of
machine stitching. This will reduce bulk when the tie is turned right side out.*

3 *Attach a safety pin to the end of the tie and
gradually push it through to turn the tie right side
out. Press the tie flat, with the seam line in the middle
of the underside.*

4 *Tuck in the raw
edges at one end of
the tie and finish by
hand with even
slipstitch (see p.138).
The raw edges at the
other end will be
concealed when the tie
is attached to the item
(see p.146). This tie
has a finished width of
¾in (2cm) and was
made from a bias-cut
strip of 2¾in (7cm).*

Making a Stiffened Tieback

A layer of buckram stiffening helps this curtain tieback keep its shape.
Attach a ring to each end and loop them onto a hook on the wall. Tiebacks can be made
from the same fabric as the curtain or a contrasting fabric.

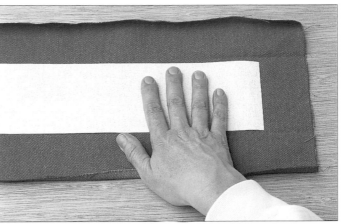

1 *Cut a piece of fabric twice the width of the finished tieback plus 1¼in (3cm). This example is 9in (23cm) wide to make a finished tie of 4in (10cm). For a one-width lined curtain, the length of the tieback should be 18in (45cm). Press ⅜in (1.5cm) to the wrong side along each long edge. Press so that the folded edges meet in the middle of the tie.*

2 *Cut a piece of buckram the finished width and length of the tieback. Place the buckram in the center of the wrong side of the tieback, aligning it with the fold lines and positioning it half the finished width of the tieback in from the end. For example, on a 4in (10cm) tie, place the buckram 2in (5cm) from the end.*

3 *Fold the fabric over the buckram and press. Sew the folded edges together with even slipstitch (see p.138).*

4 *On the underside of the tie, turn over the corners so they meet on the seam line. Turn over the point (see inset).*

5 *Fold over the end again and secure with slipstitch (see p.138) all around the folded edges. Attach a ring with couching stitch (see p.139). Repeat Steps 4 and 5 at the other end of the tieback.*

Making Corded Piping

Piping and cording are neat and attractive ways to finish edges. Piping cord is available in different thicknesses, but width No.3 and up are usually best for home furnishing uses. Make sure the piping cord is preshrunk.

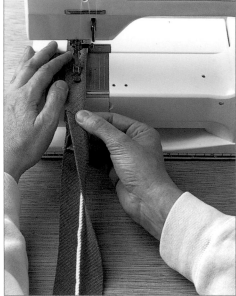

2 *Cut and join bias strips (see p.147). Wrap the piping fabric around the cord, right side out and edges matching. With a zipper foot on the machine, stitch close to the cord.*

1 *Your piping strip needs to be wide enough to leave a ⅝in (1.5cm) seam allowance beyond the piping. To work out the width of the piping strips needed, fold a corner of fabric over the piping cord and pin next to the cord. Measure ⅝in (1.5cm) out from the cord and mark a line with tailor's chalk. Trim off the excess point of fabric beyond the chalk line, unpin, and measure for the width of cording strips.*

Attaching Cording to a Curved Edge

It is not difficult to attach cording to a curved edge.
You simply need to clip the seam allowance once the cording is stitched to allow it to stretch around the curve.

1 *Place the fabric right side up with the cording on top of it, raw edges aligned. Leave about 1in (2.5cm) of cording free at the start. With a zipper foot on the machine and the needle to the left of the zipper foot, stitch close to the cording.*

2 *Once the cording is stitched, clip the seam allowance to ease the cording around the curve. On a concave curve, you can clip small triangles from the seam allowance to reduce bulk.*

Attaching Cording Around a Corner

A continuous strip of piping or cording can be attached
around all four sides of a rectangular shape by simply clipping the seam
allowance at each corner to leave a perfectly neat finish.

*Machine stitch along one side.
As you approach the corner, clip
into the seam allowance of the
cording so it opens to form a
right angle. Blunt the corner by
making a few machine stitches
across it (see clipping into
corners p.136).*

Finishing Piping

On a piped cushion, a single piece of piping or cording is
attached all around the edges of the cover. Here is a neat method of
securely joining the start and finish of the cording.

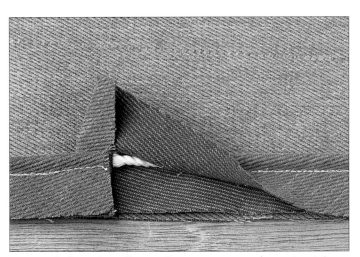

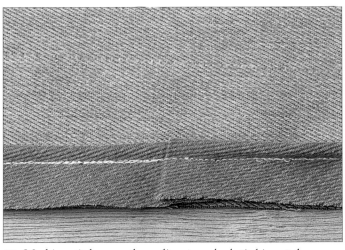

1 *Stitch the cording all around your item, stopping 2in (5cm) from
the start. Unpick a few of the stitches holding the cord at the free
end and trim the cord to butt up with the cord at the start. Fold under
½in (1cm) of fabric at the free end so the raw edge is concealed and
overlaps the raw edge of the start of the cording.*

2 *Machine stitch across the cording seam, backstitching at the
start and finish to secure firmly.*

Making Buttonholes

Buttonholes are straightforward to make using a sewing machine. If your sewing machine has a special buttonhole setting, follow the manufacturer's instructions. Otherwise, use the satin-stitch setting and follow the steps below.

1 *Mark the width of the buttons to be used with two parallel lines in tailor's chalk. Mark the positions of the buttonholes with vertical lines, which should be the diameter of the button plus ¼in (5mm). Set the stitch length on the sewing machine to just above zero and the stitch width to just below medium.*

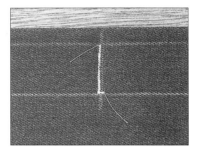

2 *With the needle to the left of the center line, stitch down one side of the buttonhole. Leave the needle in the work, raise the foot, and pivot the work 180°. Make one stitch toward the outer edge. Adjust the stitch width to its widest and make six stitches to form a bar tack at one end.*

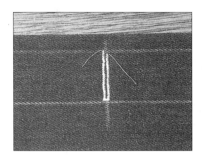

3 *Adjust the stitch width back to just below medium and stitch down the other side of the center line.*

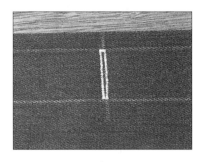

4 *With the needle in the outer, left-hand side position, adjust the stitch width to its widest again. Make six stitches to form a bar tack. Adjust the stitch width to zero and take a few stitches to finish off securely. Take threads to the back and finish off securely.*

5 *Insert a stitch ripper or the blade of a small, very sharp pair of scissors and cut the buttonhole open, being careful not to slice through the bar tacks.*

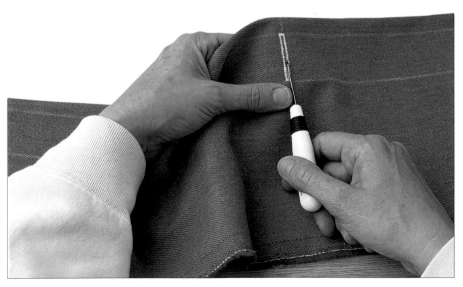

Inserting a Zipper

This is a simple, straightforward method of inserting a zipper into
the seamline of, for example, a plain pillow cover. Make sure when you choose
a zipper that it is suitable for the project style and fabric weight.

1 *Place the pieces of fabric right sides together. Center
the zipper along the fabric and mark its length – from
one stop to the other – with pins.*

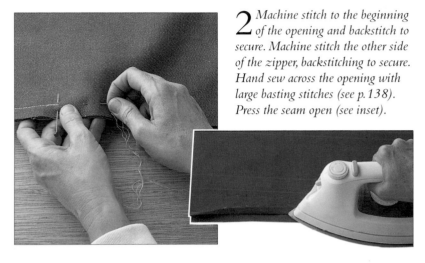

2 *Machine stitch to the beginning
of the opening and backstitch to
secure. Machine stitch the other side
of the zipper, backstitching to secure.
Hand sew across the opening with
large basting stitches (see p. 138).
Press the seam open (see inset).*

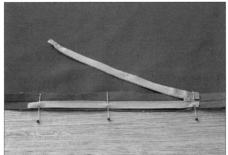

3 *Open the zipper. Place face down on the
extended seam allowance of the opening,
lining up the stop with the end of
opening. Pin one side of the zipper to the
seam allowance with teeth right on the seam.*

4 *With the zipper foot on the machine and
the needle to the left of the foot, stitch
right from the start of the zipper, keeping
close to the teeth. Backstitch at the beginning
and end to secure.*

5 *Turn the work around and extend the
other seam allowance. Close the zipper
and stitch down the other side of the zipper,
again keeping the teeth close to the center of
the seam.*

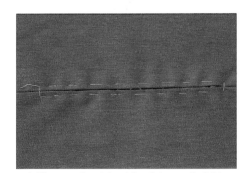

6 *Turn to the right side of the work. Using
basting stitches (see p. 138), sew around
the top, bottom, and both sides of the zipper
keeping ⅓in (7mm) from the center seam.*

7 *Using the zipper foot and with the
needle on the left-hand side of the foot,
machine stitch over the line of hand stitching,
working down one side, across the top, down
the other side, and across the bottom.*

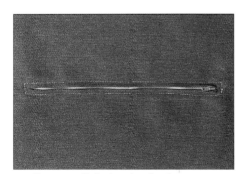

8 *Remove all the basting for the top-
stitching and from the center seam.*

Measuring and Marking Pleats

Pleats make an attractive heading for draperies. When estimating
the amount of fabric needed for curtains with a pleated heading, first consider
how full you want the finished drapes to be.

For drapes with full box-pleated heading with the whole of the width of the fabric pleated, allow 3 times the finished width. For a pleated heading with a space left between pleats, allow 2 to 2½ times the finished width. For a softly pleated heading without too much fullness, such as the café curtain on page 74, 1½ times the finished width is all that is necessary. In addition to the extra width for fullness, make an allowance for ease across the rod that holds the curtain, plus the normal seam and hem allowances for curtains, see pages 140-141.

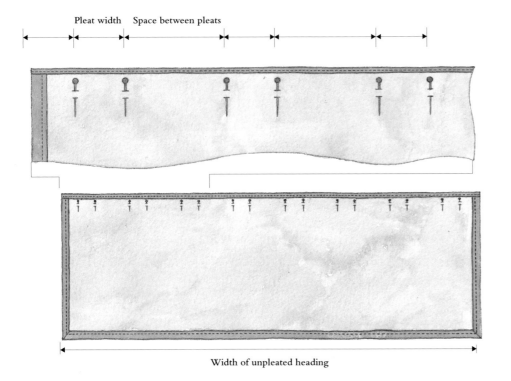

Pleat width   Space between pleats

Width of unpleated heading

1 *Once the seams and hems have been stitched, measure the width of the unpleated heading. Subtract from this the required finished width. Divide the resulting figure by the desired number of pleats – this will give you the width of fabric to form each pleat. Divide the finished width measurement by the number of spaces between the pleats – this will give you the width of each space. Working with the fabric face down, measure across the whole width of the curtain top, marking the pleat and space measurements with pins. Leave a half space at each end.*

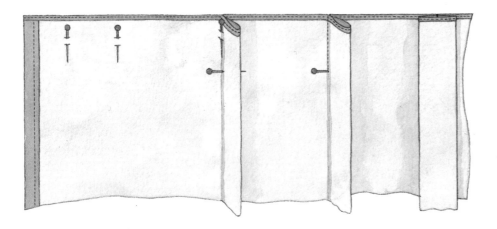

2 *Working across the curtain on the wrong side, bring the pins together to meet each other, and pin to hold the resulting pleat. Mark the base of the pleat about 3in (7.5cm) down from the top of the curtain, with a pin. Machine stitch from the top edge of the curtain, down to the marker pin, backstitching at the beginning and end to secure. Remove all pins and press the pleat flat across the back of the curtain.*

Covering Foam

Foam pads need to be covered so that they are easy to get in
and out of their outside covers. Tubes of stretchy jersey are easy to
use and can be obtained from foam suppliers.

1 *With right sides together and using a large zigzag stitch, machine stitch across one end of the jersey to make a bag.*

2 *Turn the jersey right side out so the seam is inside. Put the foam pad into the jersey bag. Pull the fabric as tight as you can and pin.*

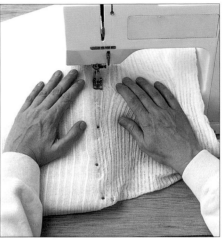

3 *Zigzag as close as possible to the edge of the pad, removing the pins as you reach them. Trim off the excess jersey. If you are covering a large piece of foam, hand sew the jersey with herringbone stitch (see p. 139).*

Softening Foam with Batting

Use a layer of 4oz (113g) synthetic batting to soften the shape
of foam and round off the squared edges. Wrap a cushion pad in batting or
apply a piece of batting to the top of a foam cube.

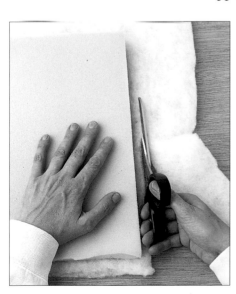

1 *Cut a piece of batting of approximately the right size to wrap around the foam pad. Place the pad on it and trim the batting to fit the pad.*

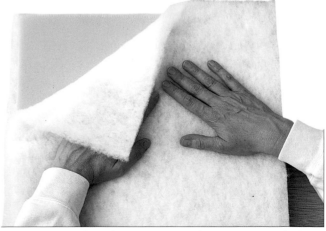

2 *Spray the surface of the batting with fabric glue. Place the foam pad on the batting and fold the rest over it. Smooth the batting into place with both hands.*

Making a Tassel from a Skein of Floss

Use a skein of embroidery floss to make this pretty
decorative tassel. Leave the paper bands in place while you make
the tassel to keep all the strands together.

1 *Pull about 8in
(20cm) or so
from the skein and
separate out two
strands. Fold them
in half and put the
looped end through
the top of the skein.
Pass the loose ends
through the loop
and pull tight.*

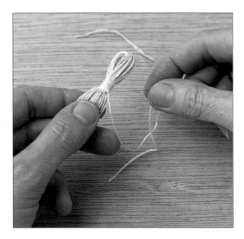

2 *Take a length of
three or four
strands of
contrasting floss.
Thread this onto a
needle and wind it
around and around
the skein about ¾in
(1.5cm) from the
top, binding in the
loose end. When the
skein is tightly
bound, sew in the
end of the thread.*

3 *Take off the paper bands and cut the end
of the skein to release the strands. Trim to
even up the ends. Comb through the tassel
with a fork to fluff it out (see inset). To attach
the tassel, thread the loose end at the top of
the tassel onto a needle. Stitch the tassel
securely in place.*

*The wide choice of colors
available in embroidery thread
means that you should have no
trouble finding exactly the right
shade to complement your fabric.*

156

Making a Tassel from Yarn or String

Any thread, from wool yarn to garden twine, can be
used to make this decorative tassel, which makes an attractive
finishing touch for a bolster.

1 *Cut a piece of cardboard the width of the needed length of the tassel. Wind the thread around the cardboard to the required thickness. Slide a separate length of thread through one end. Tie to secure.*

2 *Thread a needle with a length of contrasting thread. Wind it around and around the tassel about ¾in (1.5cm) from the top. Bind in the loose end at the start and sew in the other end when you finish.*

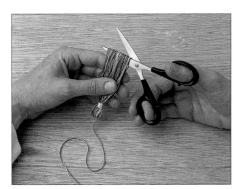

3 *Cut through the loops at the end of the tassel and trim if necessary to even them up.*

4 *Tease out the finished tassel with the end of a pin to give it fullness. Attach as for the floss tassel.*

Quilt Embellishment

This fabric disk, attached with a french knot, is a quick and easy
way of adding decoration to a quilt. Since the edges of the fabric are simply pinked,
use something that does not fray too easily.

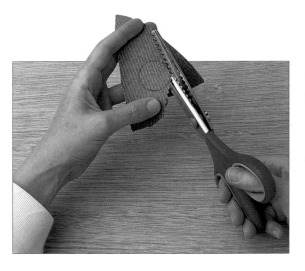

1 *You can use small scraps of fabric to make these disks. Draw around something of the required diameter, such as a coin. Cut out the disk with a pair of pinking shears.*

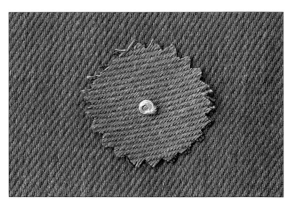

2 *Place the disk on the quilt in the marked position and attach with a french knot (see p.139) in the center of the disk.*

Paint Techniques

EQUIPMENT

You do not need a huge selection of equipment for the home improvement projects in this book, but you do need the right tools for the job if you want good results. Successful dragging, for example, is hard to achieve without a dragging brush. Always check what equipment you need and gather it all together. Otherwise, you may reach a crucial stage and find that an essential item is missing.

When painting a room, you will also need a ladder for reaching the ceiling and the tops of the walls, and a dropcloth for covering the floor and any furniture.

Basics

Buckets and paint trays
Most foam rollers come complete with paint trays. Use the ridged area of the tray for removing excess paint from the roller before painting. When painting with a brush, pour paint into a paint bucket to make the job easier. Keep a roll of cheese-cloth handy for tasks such as cleaning excess paint off your brush.

Squeegy
A rubber-edged squeegy is used to apply grout to tiles. The rubber pushes the grout between the tiles without damaging them.

Protective mask
A protective mask is an essential piece of equipment. It prevents the wearer from breathing in dust particles and fumes that may be harmful.

Small paint tray and roller

Large paint tray and roller

Protective mask

Buckets

Cheesecloth

Mask pads

Squeegy

Brushes

Basic brushes
Brushes are expensive, but try to equip yourself with at least a 4in (10cm) brush for applying paint to walls and 1in (2.5cm) and 2in (5cm) brushes for working on smaller areas, such as baseboards and details. Buy the best quality you can afford – they will last longer and shed fewer hairs while you work.

1in (2.5cm) brush

2in (5cm) brush

4in (10cm) brush

Specialized brushes
You won't need all these brushes – only those for the techniques you want to try. Stippling brushes are available in several sizes. The larger the area you are stippling, the bigger brush you will need. An artist's brush is useful for adding small details. A badger brush is used for softening glaze in techniques such as marbling.

6in (15cm) brush for colorwashing

Dragging brush

Flogging brush

Badger brush

Large stippling brush

Small stippling brush

Stencil brush

Artist's brush

Preparation

Sanding and filling

Basic equipment for preparing surfaces before painting includes steel wool, a selection of different grades of sandpaper, a putty knife, and putty. A dusting brush for wiping surfaces free of dust and a wire brush for cleaning paint brushes are also useful. You will also need a ladder and a dropcloth for covering the floor and any furniture.

Sandpaper

Steel wool

Putty

Putty knife

Wire brush

Dusting brush

Measuring, Cutting, and Gluing

Ruler and level
A good steel ruler is essential for measuring and marking your wall for projects such as stripes. A carpenter's level is invaluable for checking vertical and horizontal lines are straight. You will also need a pencil to mark lines.

Scissors and utility knife
Sharp scissors and a utility knife will be needed for stenciling and découpage, and a special mat makes the task easier.

Tape and glue
Low-impact masking tape is used for masking stripes and attaching stencils. Craft glue is used for découpage.

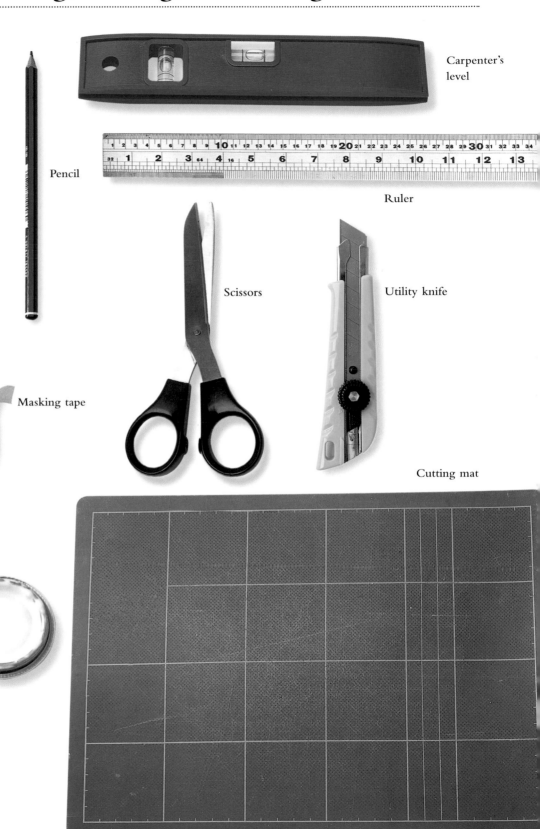

Carpenter's level

Pencil

Ruler

Scissors

Utility knife

Masking tape

Cutting mat

Glue

PAINT

Never underestimate the power of paint. With the enormous choice of colors now available, paint is the quickest and cheapest way to transform a room. Once the wall has been prepared, a simple coat of vinyl flat-finish latex is easy to apply, dries quickly, and can look great. With a little more time and effort, you can make a room something really special with a colorwash glaze, bright stripes, or a stamped pattern. A coat of paint can also help to give smaller items, such as cabinet doors, frames, and chairs, an exciting new look.

Vinyl flat latex
A water-based paint with a flat, chalky finish, vinyl latex is suitable for walls and ceilings. It is simple to apply and does not give off fumes. Vinyl latex can also be used to make a glaze.

Vinyl silk latex
A water-based paint with a slight sheen, vinyl silk is suitable for use on walls that need frequent wiping, such as kitchens and bathrooms.

Gloss
A water-based paint, vinyl gloss has a high shine and is easy to wipe clean. It can be used on walls, but it is better suited to woodwork, where it gives a long-lasting finish.

Oil eggshell
An oil-based paint with a sheen, oil eggshell is tough and durable, suitable for woodwork. Always clean your brush with turpentine after using oil-based paint.

Mixing a Glaze

A glaze for colorwash and other paint techniques can be mixed with acrylic pigment, water, and scumble glaze. You can also mix a glaze with vinyl latex, using the same proportions of scumble and water, but more paint.

1 *To mix a terra-cotta glaze, squeeze a small amount of deep red or burnt sienna artist's acrylic into a paint kettle. Add a touch of white if desired – you can use up to six colors in a glaze. Make a note of what you use in case you need to make more glaze.*

2 *Add a little water and mix the paint to a creamy consistency. Be careful not to add too much water – just enough to mix the pigment. Stir thoroughly.*

3 *Add more water and some scumble glaze in proportions of 75% glaze to 25% water. Mix well again.*

4 *If you want to make the mixture darker, add more pigment. If you want a lighter glaze, add more scumble glaze and water.*

These swatches show three variations of a terra-cotta glaze.

Light   Medium   Dark

APPLYING PAINT AND VARNISH

Paint can be applied with a roller or a brush. A roller is easier for large areas and for ceilings, but a brush often produces a better finish. Disappointing results are usually due to a lack of careful preparation and cleaning beforehand, or to overloading the brush or roller with paint – remember that using more paint does not make the work quicker.

Varnish is used to protect paintwork, particularly on items of painted furniture or on walls or doors that will receive heavy wear. Varnish is always applied with a brush, and great care must be taken to make sure the surface is evenly covered with varnish. Usually two coats are applied, and the surface should be sanded between each coat.

Applying Latex with a Brush

Always use a paint bucket and transfer paint to it from the can as you work. The bucket is safer to carry than a paint can, makes it easy to load the brush, and it won't be such a disaster if you should drop or spill it.

1 *Pour some latex into a paint bucket. Dip the tip of the brush into the paint and wipe off any excess on the side of the bucket. Never overload your brush or you will get drips and lumps on your wall.*

2 *Starting at the top right-hand corner of the wall, apply the paint in crisscrossing strokes, first one way and then the other (see inset). Keep the coverage as even as possible.*

Applying Latex with a Roller

A paint roller is easy to use. For the best results, don't overfill the tray and always be sure to slide the roller over the ridged area of the tray to remove surplus paint. Vary the direction of the roller to achieve an even coverage.

1 *Pour latex into the container part of a roller tray. Dip the roller into the paint, making sure it is evenly covered. Roll the roller over the ridged side of the tray to remove excess paint.*

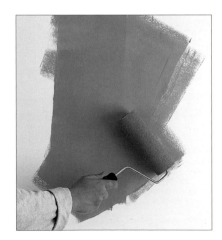

2 *Roll the paint onto the wall, working down and then off to the side. Don't just work straight up and down, or you will get stripes on the finished wall.*

166

Applying Colorwash

A colorwash glaze, applied over a coat of white vinyl
latex, gives a soft, weathered look to a wall. You can use a ready-mixed
glaze or one you have mixed yourself.

1 *Mix the glaze (see p.165). Starting at the top right-hand corner of the wall, apply the glaze with a large brush, using sweeping, crisscrossing strokes. Work in sections (see p.170).*

2 *Take the brush down from the right to the left and then turn it over and move from the left down to the right with a flowing movement. The coverage doesn't have to be even – slight variations are part of the charm of this technique.*

Applying Varnish

There are three types of varnish: flat; satin, which has a slight sheen; and gloss,
which has a pronounced shine. Acrylic varnish can be used for most purposes, but polyurethane
varnish is best for areas that will have very heavy wear, such as painted floors.

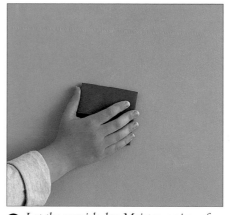

1 *Pour some varnish into a paint bucket and stir it thoroughly. Using a brush, apply one coat, making sure the whole area is covered evenly and completely.*

2 *Let the varnish dry. Moisten a piece of waterproof abrasive paper and start to rub all over the varnished surface with small circular movements. Make sure any uneven areas are thoroughly smoothed.*

3 *Apply a second coat of varnish as before. If more coats are needed, sand the surface between each coat.*

PREPARATION

Walls and other surfaces must be properly prepared before painting or you will not get good results. Give walls a thorough wash, sand with abrasive paper, and fill any cracks with putty. Strip off any old wallpaper with a steam stripper or solvents. If walls are in particularly bad shape, they might need to be refinished before you paint. Any new plaster should be left to dry out thoroughly – at least a month – before painting.

Preparing Furniture

Old paint and varnish must be removed before furniture is painted if your new treatment
is to look good and last. Be very careful when using a chemical stripper; always wear a mask. New
objects need little preparation other than sanding to remove any rough areas.

1 *Use chemical stripper to remove old paint and varnish. Wearing thick rubber gloves, apply stripper over the surface with a paintbrush. Use an old toothbrush to get into the crevices of molded surfaces (inset). Leave the stripper on until the old coat has bubbled up.*

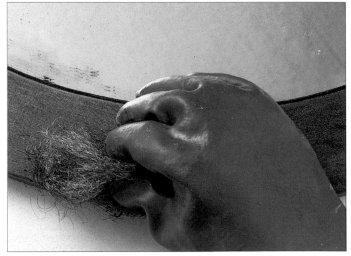

2 *Remove the softened paint or varnish with coarse and then fine steel wool, rubbing it all over the surface. If necessary, repeat the process with a second coat of stripper.*

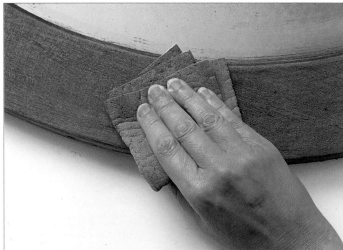

3 *Wipe off the excess stripper with an absorbent cloth and the neutralizer recommended by your product. If you are applying water-based varnish, do not use turpentine.*

Preparing Walls

Bad cracks on walls should be carefully filled before painting.
Any loose plaster should be removed and the crack filled and sanded
to make a smooth, clean surface for painting.

1 *Using a sharp pointed tool such as a screwdriver, dig out the loose plaster from the crack. Brush away any particles.*

2 *Using a trowel, lay a generous amount of putty over the crack. Cover about 18in (45cm) at a time.*

3 *With the flat edge of the trowel, work the putty into the crack, pulling the trowel down to make a smooth surface.*

4 *Let the plaster dry completely, then sand the surface with fine-grit sandpaper wrapped around a block of wood. Sand until you can no longer feel bumps when you run your hand over the area.*

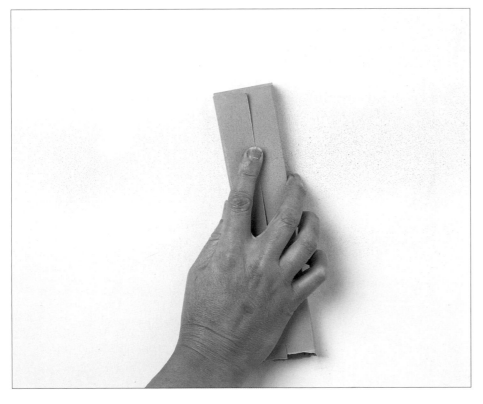

ORDER OF WORK

The order in which you work is an important part of successful home decorating. When painting a room, start with the ceiling. Then paint walls, window frames, doors, and base boards. Start at the top right-hand corner of the wall that contains the door into the room. The reason for this is, in theory, by the time you reach the wall opposite the door – the wall you see as you come into the room – you will have perfected your technique. When glazing a wall, it is best to work in irregularly shaped sections to avoid leaving obvious joined-up lines.

Glazing a Wall in Sections

When applying glaze to a wall for paint effects, you need to work quickly so the edge of one section does not dry before you move onto the next, leaving telltale join-up marks. Working irregular areas helps to make joins hard to see.

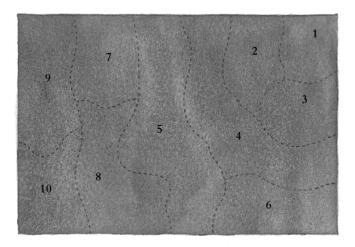

Do not work in regular blocks. Some of the edges will dry before you can get back to them, and the regularity of the shapes will make joined-up lines very obvious. This diagram shows a good way of working in sections so you get back to the wet edges quickly. The irregularity of the shapes makes it hard for the eye to spot any joined areas.

Painting a Fireplace

Always work from the inside to the outside when you paint a fireplace, whether you are simply giving it a coat of paint or applying glaze or paint effects such as marbling.

Although you may only want to apply the main decorative technique to the mantlepiece and outer section, do not ignore the rest of the fireplace. It is important that the whole fireplace is cleaned and painted; otherwise, the inner areas will look scruffy beside the newly painted mantlepiece and detract from the new effect.

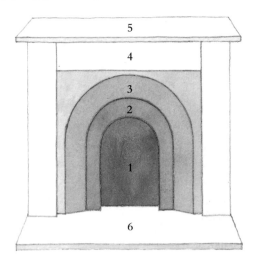

Key to order of work

1 Inside of fireplace

2 Inner section

3 Middle section

4 Outer section

5 Mantlepiece

6 Hearth

Painting a Door

Whatever style of door you are painting, always start at
the top of the door and work down. A paneled door should be painted in
sections, in the order shown below.

First remove the door handles and other hardware such as keyhole and finger plates. Sand the door and thoroughly clean the surface to remove all dust particles.

If any patches of wood appear after sanding, apply primer paint to the exposed wood and let it dry before proceeding with the paint treatment.

On a paneled door, start by painting the panels and moldings and then move on to the horizontal and vertical stiles. Make sure that paint does not collect in the corners of the moldings and drip down the door.

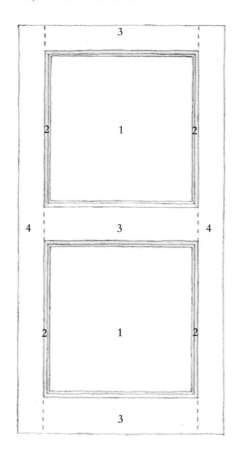

Key to order of work

1 Panels

2 Moldings

3 Horizontal stiles

4 Vertical stiles

Cleaning Brushes

Look after your brushes and they will last longer
and give better results. Always clean them as soon as possible
after you finish painting.

When you finish work, clean your brushes immediately. With water-based paints, put the brush into warm water with some liquid detergent. Using a wire brush, stroke through the bristles firmly to remove any remaining paint. If paint has been allowed to harden, soften it with denatured alcohol before using the wire brush. Rinse the brush thoroughly in clean water.

For brushes used with oil-based paint, clean with turpentine first and then wash in warm water and detergent. Rinse all brushes well and leave them to dry in a warm place, keeping the bristles straight.

CUTTING STENCILS, COMBS, AND ROLLERS

Stencils, bought or homemade, cardboard combs, and cut foam rollers are quick and easy ways of applying pattern and decoration to your walls, and all are simple to make. When cutting these items, always use a new blade in your utility knife and change it regularly – a blunt blade will not produce clean results.

Stencils can be made from paper or cardboard, but acetate is an ideal choice. It is strong and easy to clean, and you can see through it, which makes it easier to position repeating designs on the wall.

Combs and rollers are even easier to make. For the comb, notched teeth are cut out of a piece of stiff cardboard. The comb is then dragged through wet paint to produce a combed pattern. For a quick way of painting stripes, cut a section out of a foam roller. The remaining raised areas produce two stripes with each stroke of the roller.

Making a Stencil

Whether the design is simple or complex, the method is much the same.
Draw or trace a design, transfer it to cardboard or acetate and cut out the stencil.
You can then apply the stencil to the wall with paint.

1 *Draw or trace the shape you want to use on a piece of paper. If you haven't stenciled before, keep to simple shapes.*

2 *Take a piece of acetate and place it over the drawing. Trace the image very carefully with a permanent marker pen.*

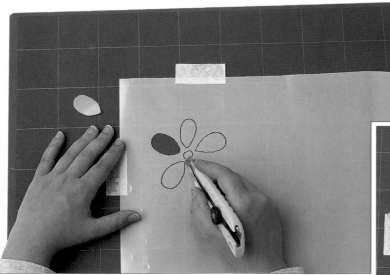

3 *Place the acetate with the traced image on a cutting board or other surface you can cut on and attach it with masking tape. Using a utility knife, carefully cut inside the lines marking the shape to produce the finished stencil (see inset).*

Making a Comb

Use sturdy, firm cardboard to make this comb. Cut the cardboard deep
enough to provide a good "handle" for the comb. Don't worry if your "teeth" are not
perfectly even – any irregularities will not be obvious in the final technique.

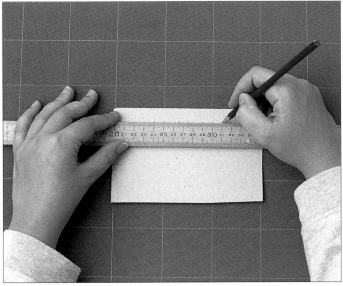

1 *Use a piece of sturdy cardboard measuring approximately 6in (15cm) wide by 4in (10cm) deep. Using a pencil and ruler and working about ¾in (2cm) down from the top, mark the card at ½in (1cm) intervals. Decrease this to ¼in (5mm) at the center of the card for a fraction of an inch and then increase to ½in (1cm) again.*

2 *Draw diagonal lines from each marked point to the edge of the cardboard. Shade in the areas where the lines cross. These will form the "teeth" of your comb.*

3 *Using a sharp utility knife and holding the cardboard steady on a cutting mat, cut out the shaded areas to form the "teeth" of the comb.*

Cutting a Roller for Stripes

An attractive striped effect is easy to achieve with a specially
cut foam roller. Some of the foam is cut away, leaving the remaining surface to
create two stripes with each stroke.

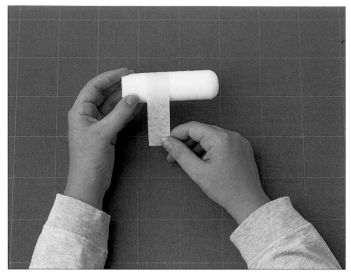

1 *Take a small paint roller, measuring about 4¼in (11cm), and
remove the foam pad. Place a strip of masking tape all the way
around the roller. The distance between the tape and the end of the
roller should be the same as the width of the tape.*

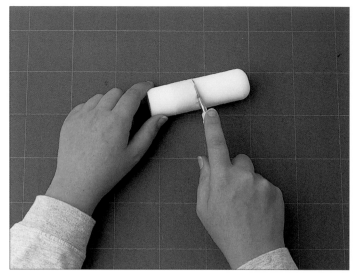

2 *Cut into the foam on each side of the tape, cutting right down to
the core of the roller. Cut all around the roller in this way.*

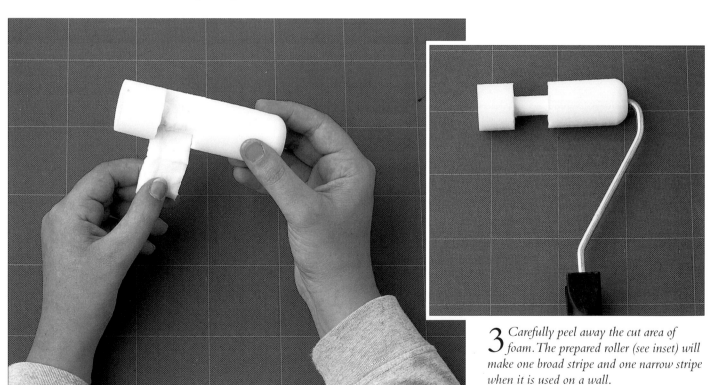

3 *Carefully peel away the cut area of
foam. The prepared roller (see inset) will
make one broad stripe and one narrow stripe
when it is used on a wall.*

MEASURING AND MASKING

Before starting projects such as stripes, stone blocks, or trompe l'oeil panels, it is important to measure the wall carefully and mark the design. Don't be tempted just to start painting and hope for the best. For stripes, for example, measure the height and width of the walls, decide on the width of stripe you want, and make sure this works, adjusting the size of the stripe if necessary. Don't worry if one stripe has to be slightly smaller than the others – no one else will notice. When marking stripes or masking areas, always use low-impact masking tape – normal tape is likely to pull away paint as you remove it from the wall.

Bear in mind that room measurements are rarely completely regular. You will probably find the baseboard varies slightly in depth, or your wall is slightly higher at one end than the other. Take these differences into account when you are marking the design.

Measuring and Painting Stripes

Stripes are easy to do if they are carefully measured and marked on your wall.
First decide on the width of your stripe – the horizontal stripes here measure 8in (20cm) deep.
Measure the depth of your wall to make sure the stripe fits and adjust it if necessary.

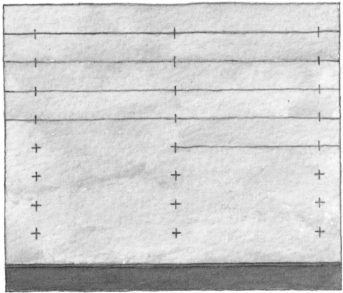

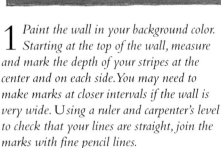

1 *Paint the wall in your background color. Starting at the top of the wall, measure and mark the depth of your stripes at the center and on each side. You may need to make marks at closer intervals if the wall is very wide. Using a ruler and carpenter's level to check that your lines are straight, join the marks with fine pencil lines.*

2 *Every other stripe will be painted in the contrasting color. Apply low-impact masking tape to the outside of the pencil lines to mark every other stripe. Apply paint to the taped stripes, making sure you work right up to the tape to give a straight edge each time. Remove the masking tape when the stripes are complete. Check that the paint has not bled under the tape.*

Working around obstacles

In every room, stripes or checks will meet windows, doors, and other obstacles. Don't worry about these. Just let the lines continue as they fall down or run across the wall. The finished effect will look all the more natural.

Marking Stone Blocks

Make sure the size of the blocks is related to the size of the wall or room.
For a wall that is 8ft (2.5m) high, for example, blocks of 12in (30cm) deep and 24in (60cm)
wide look good. The higher the room, the larger the blocks should be.

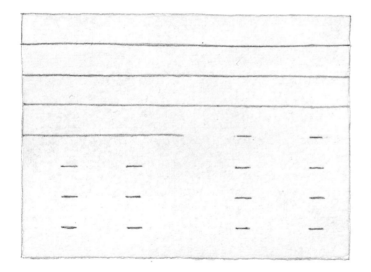

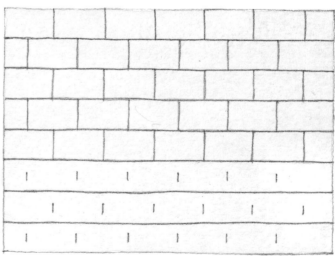

1 *Divide the wall into equal 12in (30cm) spaces and mark in pencil as shown. Make several marks at intervals across the wall. Using the marks as a guide, draw lines right across the wall with a level or ruler. Starting from the top right corner of the wall, mark the width of the blocks at 24in (60cm) intervals. Don't worry if they are slightly smaller at the corners.*

2 *Draw the vertical lines for the top row of blocks with a ruler. Use this as a guide for the remaining blocks. The second line should be staggered as shown, so start with a half block. The third line should be the same as the first and so on.*

Marking Trompe L'oeil Panels

Trompe l'oeil panels can be made on walls or flat doors. A long wall looks best broken into
three panels. On a shorter wall, make two panels of equal size. The panels here measure 24 x 32in (60 x 80cm),
with 12in (30cm) between each panel, but you can adapt the size to suit your wall.

1 *Calculate the total area of the panels from top to bottom and from the outside edge of the right-hand panel to the outside edge of the panel on the left. Center this area on your wall about 4in (10cm) up from the dado and mark it in pencil.*

2 *Mark the center point of the center panel. Mark the sides of the center panel. Mark the inside edges of the left and right panels and draw in vertical lines. Use a carpenter's level to make sure your lines are straight.*

3 *Remove the line at the center of the panels and the horizontal marks between the panels. The panels are now ready for painting (see p.36).*

Marking a Wall for Stamping

Decide on how much space you want between each stamp on the wall. Bear in
mind that if the stamps are too close together, the wall will look very busy. Here the stamps
are 24in (60cm) apart and the horizontal rows are 32in (80cm) apart.

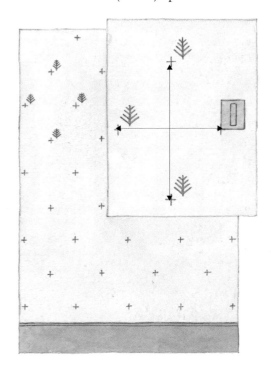

Mark the position of each stamp very lightly in pencil on the wall with a cross. Stagger the horizontal rows as shown so that each stamp in the second row comes halfway between two in the first row and so on. When stamping the wall, place the bottom left corner of the stamp in the angle of the cross marking the position. This will mean that stamps are evenly positioned.

177

TEMPLATES AND STENCILS

The templates shown here are for use with the projects in the first part of this book. All are simple shapes, easy to trace or copy. If you want to make any of the templates bigger or smaller than illustrated, you can enlarge or reduce them on a photocopier or by copying them on to squared paper. You may, for example, prefer to use a smaller version of the heart shape for gilding or to appliqué a series of diamond shapes onto your bed linen. The stencils shown on pages 183–185 are not the exact designs used in the projects, but provide a range of attractive ideas for use in your home.

Umbrella Stand Template

This diamond template is used for the gilded umbrella stand (see pp.20–21). Simple shapes like this work best with such a glamorous technique. To use the design at this size, simply trace over it, attach the design to the item, and go over the line with pencil to transfer the outline to the wood.

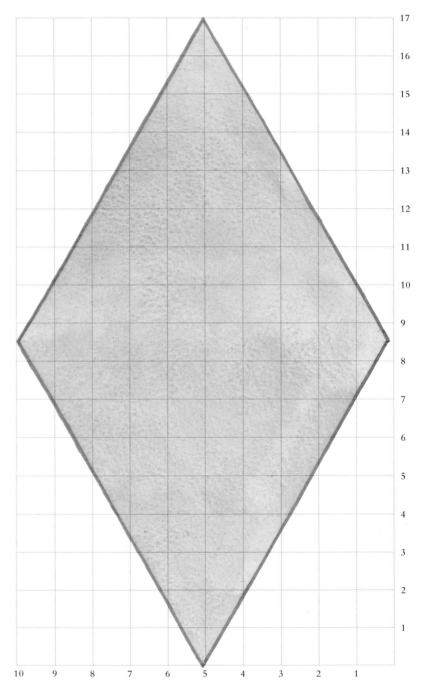

Valance Template

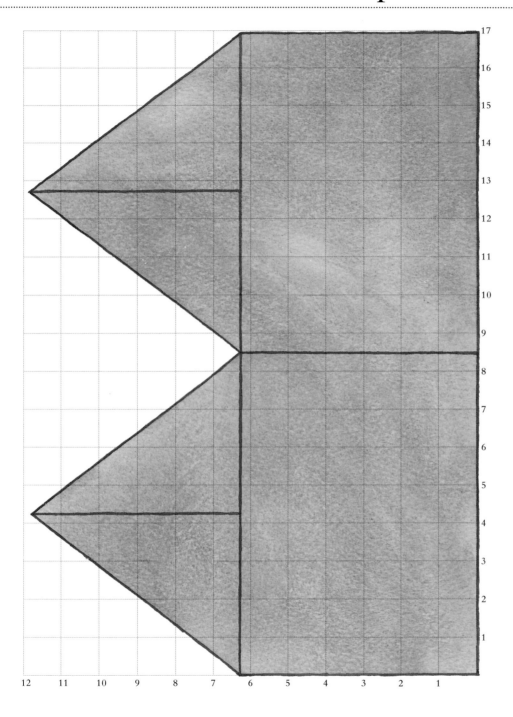

Each section of this template should be 6in (15cm) wide to fit the width of a finished panel of the valance (see pp.64–65). Photocopy the template, enlarging it by 75%. Attach the template to a piece of cardboard and cut around it, or trace the design onto the cardboard. The cardboard is then used to cut the valance to shape.

Heart-shaped Template and Leaf Template

This template is used for the headboard cover featured on pp.104–105. Trace the heart shape and cut it out. Then place the shape onto the fusible webbing used in the project and draw around it. Use the shape the size it is here or enlarge it on a photocopier or onto squared paper to suit the size of your headboard cover.

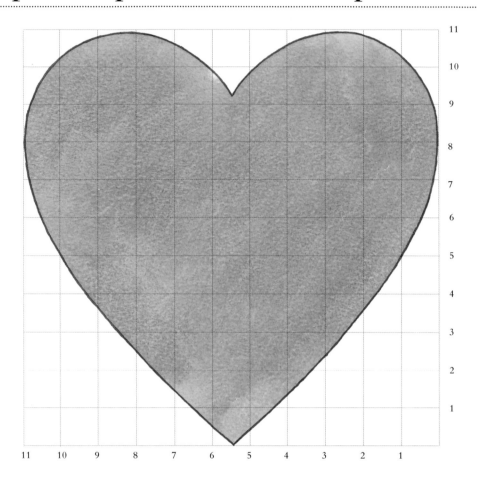

This simple leaf shape (below) is used to appliqué the bed linen shown on pp.94–95. Trace the leaf shape shown here and cut it out. Place the shape onto the fusible webbing and draw around it to make as many leaves as required.

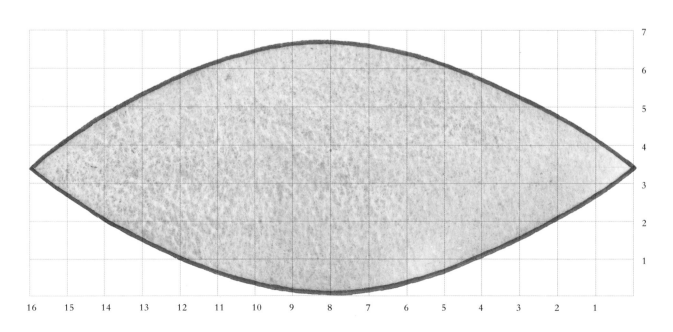

180

Shower Curtain Template

This template is used to create the lacy-look edging to the shower curtain on pp.116–117. To use at the same size as shown in the project, enlarge the template by 50% on a photocopier or size up using squared paper. Transfer the design onto a piece of card and cut out the shape. Finally make the holes with a hole punch.

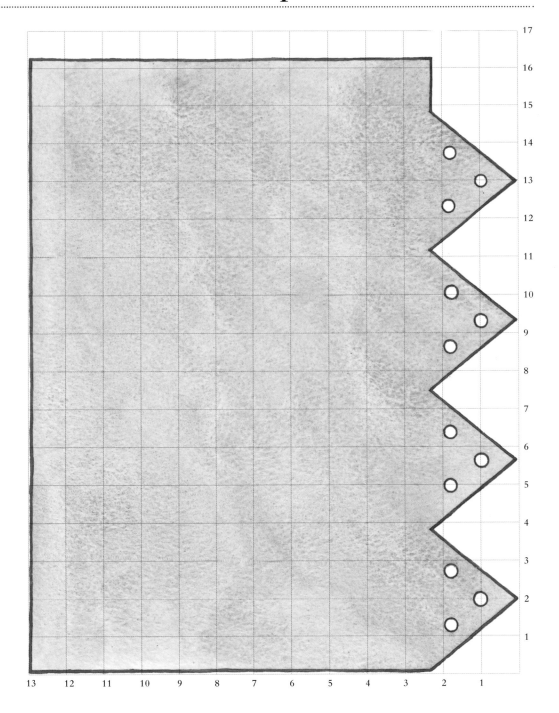

Topiary Templates

These simple templates help you make the spectacular mural on pp.88–89. You will need to enlarge the templates on a photocopier to make them big enough. Copy them in several sections onto A3 paper to make a finished image of about 32in (80cm) high. Then follow the instructions on p.89.

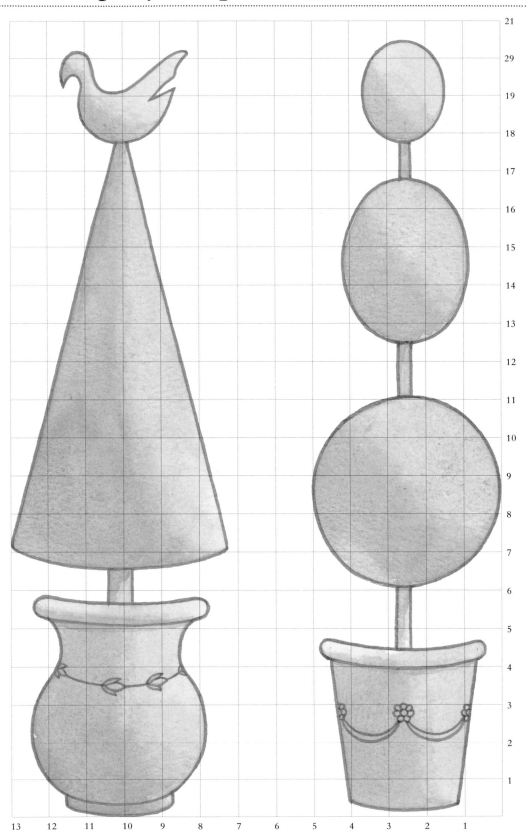

Bedroom Stencils

These stencil designs can be used to create the bedroom wall border on pp.96–97. To use any of these designs, trace the shape, working around all the shaded areas. Transfer the outline tracing to stencil cardboard or acetate, shading the blocks to guide you as you cut. Carefully cut out all the shaded areas, keeping the areas in between them intact. For more details, see p.172.

Kitchen Stencils

These charming fruit and vegetable designs can be used to give a new look to kitchen tiles (see pp.76–77). To keep the stenciling simple, the two colors in each design are used in separate areas. For further details on making a stencil, see p.172.

Bathroom Stencils

For the frosted glass panel (see pp.122–123), stencils are used in a different way. Instead of cutting away the shaded areas, you cut around them. The resulting shapes are then attached to the glass and the frosting is sprayed over them. The shapes are then removed to reveal the unfrosted glass beneath and the pattern created by the cut-out areas in each design.

INDEX

GLOSSARY

Soft furnishing terms

Awl A pointed tool used to make the holes for screw eyes in a wooden batten.
Batten A piece of wood, usually 1 x 2in (2 x 5cm) to which the top of a shade is fixed. The batten is then attached to the wall, window frame, or ceiling.
Batting A material used for softening shapes, such as a cube cushion, or for padding an item like a headboard cover.
Bias-cut Fabric cut on the bias is cut across the vertical and horizontal grain. Fabric cut in this way molds around curves and corners more easily than fabric cut on the grain. Bias-cut strips are therefore used for piping, corded piping, and for ties that are to be made into bows.
Café clip A decorative clip used to hold the top of a café curtain and attach it to the curtain pole.
Cleat A metal hook that is attached to one side of a window and used to secure the cords of a shade when it is raised.
Corded piping A neat finish used on cushions and other furnishings made from strips of fabric cut on the bias and wrapped around lengths of cord.
Cording An arrangement of cords threaded through rings at the back of a shade enabling it to be raised and lowered.
Dowel A slender wooden rod inserted into a fabric pocket at the back of a roman shade. This helps to pull the shade up neatly.
Jersey A fine, stretchy fabric used for covering foam cushion pads. This makes it easier to take the pads in and out of their outside covers.
Drop weight A wooden or brass holder through which the ends of the shade cording are threaded.
Mitering A method of making a neat corner where a side hem and base hem meet.
Punch and dye set This punches a hole in fabric and fits the two parts of a metal eyelet, one on each side of the fabric.
Recess window A window that is set back into the wall. A curtain or shade can be hung inside or outside the recess.
Return The part of a curtain or shade that goes around the end of a track and batten. When measuring for fabric requirements, remember to include the return.
Selvedge The edge of fabric formed in the weaving process. It often shrinks during the life of a curtain so should be completely removed if possible.
Tieback A tie used to hold back a curtain. A tieback can be made from fabric strengthened with fabric stiffener, or from rope or cord.

Paint terms

Architrave The wooden molding around a door or window.
Badger brush A brush used for softening glaze in techniques such as marbling.
Cheesecloth Cotton cloth usually supplied in a roll and used for many purposes such as ragging and softening brushmarks on a colorwash.
Colorwashing A simple paint technique in which a coat of glaze is applied with rough crisscrossing strokes over a vinyl latex base.
Dado A thin wooden molding that runs around a wall at about the height of an upright chair.
Découpage A decorative technique using a number of cutout pictures to cover a surface. The images are stuck down on an object or wall and varnished.
Dragging A decorative paint effect in which a dragging brush is dragged down a glazed wall leaving the impressions of the fine bristles.
Glaze A translucent mixture made from acrylic pigment, water, and scumble glaze and used for decorative paint effects. Glaze can also be mixed with vinyl latex, scumble glaze, and water, or bought ready-mixed.
Gloss A water-based paint with a high shine that is easy to wipe clean. It is most suitable for woodwork where it gives a long-lasting finish.
Grouting A special fine plaster used for filling in the spaces between tiles.
Marbling A decorative paint technique that imitates marble. Fine lines representing the veins in marble are painted over a softened glaze.

Oil eggshell An oil-based paint with a sheen to the finish. Tough and durable, eggshell is suitable for woodwork.
Squeegy A rubber-edged tool used for applying grout to tiles.
Stippling A decorative paint effect in which a box-like bristle brush is dabbed over a glazed wall, lifting the glaze slightly and leaving the impression of the bristles.
Tortoiseshell A decorative finish that imitates a tortoise's shell and can be used on small items such as lamp bases and boxes. The item is painted in warm yellow and given a coat of wood stain. Markings imitating those on a tortoise's shell are then added in acrylic paint.
Trompe l'oeil A technique that uses painted shadow lines to make a flat area look three-dimensional.
Varnish A resinous solution applied to protect paintwork. There are three types of finish – flat; satin, which has slight sheen; and gloss, which has a pronounced shine. Acrylic varnish is suitable for most purposes, but polyurethane varnish is best for areas that will have very heavy wear, such as floors.
Vinyl flat latex A water-based paint with a flat, chalky finish, suitable for decorating walls and ceilings.
Vinyl silk latex A water-based paint with a slight sheen to the finish. This is suitable for walls that need frequent wiping, such as kitchens and bathrooms.
Woodgraining A decorative technique used for making cheap wood or board look as if it is made of mahogany, oak, or other quality material. The item is painted pale yellow and given a coat of glaze. The glaze is then dragged and softened and appropriate knot and grain marks are added with the tip of a sharpened cork.

SUPPLIERS

Fabric

American Discount Wall and Window Coverings
1411 Fifth Avenue
Pittsburgh, PA 15219
Tel: (800) 777-2737
Custom upholstery and decorator fabrics.

Hancock's
3841 Hinkleville Road
Paducah KY 42001
Tel: (800) 845-8723
Decorator fabric and upholstery.

Paints

Tower Paint and Decorating
PO Box 2345
Oshkosh, WI 54903-2345
Tel: (920) 235-6520
www.towerpaint.com
Offering paints and decorating supplies.

Edwards Paint and Decorating Center
19 Glennie Street
Worcester, MA 01605
Tel: (800) 893-3732
www.edwardspaint.com
Specializing in paint, wallpaper, and floorcovering.

Kent Paint and Decorating
Route 341 East
Kent CT
Tel: (860) 927-4478
www.kentpaint.com
Providing paint and other supplies.

Pearl Paints
308 Canal Street
New York, NY 10013
Tel: (800) 221-6845
www.pearlpaint.com
Fine paints and art supplies

Blank Furniture

Mark Sales Co Inc
151-20 88th Street
Suite 2G
Queens, NY 11414
Tel: (718) 835-9319
Imported, unfinished wood furniture.

Mosaic

Norberry Tile
207 2nd Avenue South
Seattle, WA 98104
Tel: (206) 343-9916
www.norberrytile.com
Custom made slate, stone, and mosaic tiles.

Olla Linda
7010-E Burnet Road
Austin, TX 78757
Tel: (512) 458-6422
www.importgallery.com
Importer of Mexican mosaic tiles.

Mosaic House Moroccan Imports
62 W 22nd Street
New York, NY 10010
Tel: (212) 414-2525
Importer of fine mosaic tiles.

Stencils

Stenciler's Emporium
1325 Armstrong Road
Suite 170
Northfield, MN 55057
Tel: (800) 229-1760
www.stencilers.com
Decorative stencils and related supplies.

Stencil Ease
PO Box 1127
Old Saybrook, CT 06475
Tel: (800) 334-1776
www.stencilease.com
Home decor, stencils, and accessories.

Furniture and Accessories

Arroyo Design
224 North Fourth Avenue
Tucson, AZ 85705
Tel: (602) 884-1012
Custom mesquite furniture; call for catalog.

Crate and Barrel
Tel: (888) 249-4158
www.crateandbarrel.com
Home furnishings and equipment. Call for catalog.

IKEA
Tel: (800) 434-4532
Regional
Tel: (800) 931-8940 East Coast
Tel: (800) 912-1199 West Coast
www.ikea-usa.com
Call for catalog.

Neiman Marcus
PO Box 650589
Dallas, TX 75265-0589
Tel: (800) 825-8000
Call for catalog.

New West
211 Big Horn Avenue
Cody, WY 82414
Tel: (800) 853-4234
Custom Western style furnishings. Call for catalog.

Pier 1 Imports
Tel: (800) 477-4371
www.pier1.com
Call for retail store locations.

Pottery Barn
Mail Order Department
PO Box 7044
San Francisco, CA 94120
Tel: (800) 922-5507
Call for catalog and store locations.

ACKNOWLEDGMENTS

The publishers would like to thank the following companies for kindly supplying materials and items for use in photography for this book.

Antiques The Antique Trader, Chairworks, Compton Antiques, The Long Room, The Old Cinema, 243.
Fabric and paint Anna French, The Cloth Shop, The Decorative Fabrics Gallery, Designers Guild, Farrow & Ball, Fired Earth, Jane Churchill, Leyland Paints from Nuline, Melin Tregwynt, Mulberry Design Company, Osborne & Little, Paint Magic, Ottilie Stevenson, Ruffle & Hook.
Flooring Amtico, Crucial Trading, Roger Oates Design, The Rug Company, Stone Age.
Furniture Angraves Cane Furniture, Aero, alphabeds, Freud, Hitch Mylius Interiors Bis, Nordic Style, Purves & Purves, Royal Arrow, SCP, Shaker, Soo San.
Home accessories Acquisitions (Fireplaces) Ltd, Agnes B, Anthony Redmile, The Bradley Collection, Christopher Wray Lighting, Divertimenti Retail Ltd, Floris, Imperial Towel Rails, The Laundry, Neal Street East, Neal's Yard Remedies, Nicole Farhi Home, Ocean Home Shopping, The Pot Company, Quintessa Art Collection, Samuel Heath & Sons, A Touch of Brass, The White Company.
General stores B&Q, Habitat, Laura Ashley, John Lewis, Liberty, Sainsbury's Homebase, Wickes.
Miscellaneous Adolfo Dominguez, Ariel Crittall, Arthur Beale, The Camden Garden Centre, David Armstrong Designs, James Smith & Sons, Soho Shoes, Wallace & Sewell, Wheatley's Flowers.

Author's Acknowledgments

Gina Moore would like to thank the following for kindly supplying fabric:
Ian Mankin Contrast-lined Door Curtain, Café Curtain, Child's Quilt, Lined Baskets, Bench Cushion, Bathroom Organiser.
Osborne and Little Console Table Cover, Director's Chair.
Romo Fabric Blind with Ties, Roman Blind, Cube Footstool, Throw.
James Brindley of Harrogate Pleated Curtains with Pelmet.
Henry Bertrand Envelope Cushions.
Cath Kidston Table Napkins and Place Mats.
Otillie Stevenson Tie-on Seat Cushions, Bolster Cushion.
Designers Guild Bed Canopy, Bathroom Organiser.
Mulberry Roller Blind.

Amy Dawson would like thank the following for kindly supplying paints and other materials:
Harvey Baker Design Ltd, The Mosaic Workshop, Annie Sloan Paints, Askew Paint Centre, Paper and Paints, Farrow and Ball, The Painted Finish

Gina and Amy would also like to thank Lucinda Symons, Brian Hatton, Sam Lloyd and everyone at the studio, Ali Edney for great style, Steve Gott for building the sets, everyone at C&B Packaging particularly Helen Collins, and last, but not least, our editor Jinny Johnson for all her help and patience.

NOTES